Knowing

God's

Voice

HARVESTIME INTERNATIONAL INSTITUTE

This course is part of the **Harvestime International Institute**, a program designed to equip believers for effective spiritual harvest.

The basic theme of the training is to teach what Jesus taught, that which took men who were fishermen, tax collectors, etc., and changed them into reproductive Christians who reached their world with the Gospel in a demonstration of power.

This manual is a single course in one of several modules of curriculum which moves believers from visualizing through deputizing, multiplying, organizing, and mobilizing to achieve the goal of evangelizing.

© Harvestime International Institute
http://www.harvestime.org

TABLE OF CONTENTS

HOW TO USE THIS MANUAL

MANUAL FORMAT

Each lesson consists of:

Objectives: These are the goals you should achieve by studying the chapter. Read them before starting the lesson.

Key Verse: This verse emphasizes the main concept of the chapter. Memorize it.

Chapter Content: Study each section. Use your Bible to look up any references not printed in the manual.

Self-Test: Take this test after you finish studying the chapter. Try to answer the questions without using your Bible or this manual. When you have concluded the Self-Test, check your answers in the answer section provided at the end of the book.

For Further Study: This section will help you continue your study of the Word of God, improve your study skills, and apply what you have learned to your life and ministry.

Final Examination: If you are enrolled in this course for credit, you received a final examination along with this course. Upon conclusion of this course, you should complete this examination and return it for grading as instructed.

ADDITIONAL MATERIALS NEEDED

You will need a King James version of the Bible.

SUGGESTIONS FOR GROUP STUDY

FIRST MEETING

Opening: Open with prayer and introductions. Get acquainted and register the students.

Establish Group Procedures: Determine who will lead the meetings, the time, place, and dates for the sessions.

Praise And Worship: Invite the presence of the Holy Spirit into your training session.

Distribute Manuals To Students: Introduce the manual title, format, and course objectives provided in the first few pages of the manual.

Make The First Assignment: Students will read the chapters assigned and take the Self-Tests prior to the next meeting. The number of chapters you cover per meeting will depend on chapter length, content, and the abilities of your group.

SECOND AND FOLLOWING MEETINGS

Opening: Pray. Welcome and register any new students and give them a manual. Take attendance. Have a time of praise and worship.

Review: Present a brief summary of what you studied at the last meeting.

Lesson: Discuss each section of the chapter using the **HEADINGS IN CAPITAL BOLD FACED LETTERS** as a teaching outline. Ask students for questions or comments on what they have studied. Apply the lesson to the lives and ministries of your students.

Self-Test: Review the Self-Tests students have completed. (Note: If you do not want the students to have access to the answers to the Self-Tests, you may remove the answer pages from the back of each manual.)

For Further Study: You may do these projects on a group or individual basis.

Final Examination: If your group is enrolled in this course for credit, you received a final examination with this course. Reproduce a copy for each student and administer the exam upon conclusion of this course.

INTRODUCTION

"What is God's will for me?"

This question is perhaps the one most often asked by believers. It is also a question that frequently confronts Christian leaders as men and women turn to them for guidance in decision making.

In everyday situations of life, believers are constantly making choices which determine whether or not they will do the perfect will of God. It is essential to know God's voice, understand His will, and make right decisions each day. It is important because each minor decision affects the finding of God's will for a lifetime.

Man must make choices in relationship to God's will. This plan was instituted by God when Adam and Eve were placed in the Garden of Eden (Genesis 1-3). God's will for Adam and Eve was to name the animals, tend the Garden, have companionship with each other, and reproduce to populate the earth. Most important, they were to maintain intimate fellowship with God. Adam and Eve were also warned about what was <u>not</u> God's will. They were forbidden to eat of the tree of the knowledge of good and evil.

Including the story of Adam and Eve, the entire Bible is a history of decisions which individuals and nations made in relation to God's will. You can learn from both the successes and failures of these men and women.

One of the most exciting revelations in the Bible is that God has a definite plan for every individual for this life and eternity. In order to fulfill these plans you must come to know God's voice. You must learn how He has communicated in times past and how He speaks today.

This course explains how God speaks to man and how to find God's will for your life. Guidelines are given on knowing the voice of God and determining His will. The pattern of God's will and Scriptural examples of how God reveals His will are discussed.

A Scriptural model for decision making is explained. Guidelines are presented on overcoming wrong decisions, what to do if you have missed the will of God, and handling questionable practices. Six stages of revelation of a plan of God are also identified.

Harvestime International Institute curriculum focuses on what Jesus taught to equip men and women to reach their world with the Gospel. One of the great truths He revealed was that God does speak to men:

I am the good shepherd and know my sheep, and am known of mine. . .

And other sheep I have which are not of this fold: them also I must bring, and they shall hear my voice, and there shall be one fold and one shepherd.

My sheep hear my voice, and I know them, and they follow me. (John 10:14,16,27)

God has a plan for intimate relationship with mankind. Man is known by God and can know Him personally.

You *can* know the voice of God!

COURSE OBJECTIVES

Upon completion of this course you will be able to:

- Explain the relationship between knowing God's voice and determining His will.

- Discuss the importance of knowing God's will.

- Explain how God reveals His will.

- Understand the will of God as revealed in Scriptures.

- Determine the will of God in matters not specifically dealt with in Scriptures.

- Use Scriptural methods of decision making.

- Correct wrong decisions.

- Explain the six stages of revelation.

- Share with others the Biblical guidelines for knowing God's voice.

PERSONAL OBJECTIVES

Because this course deals with knowing God's voice and His will, it is suggested that you set personal objectives for the study. Your objectives might be to determine God's will in a specific matter, find God's answer for a problem, or determine God's will for your life's work and ministry. List your personal objectives in the space provided below. As you study, apply what you learn to each problem you listed.

Complete this sentence: "I want to hear God's voice and know His will about. . . "

_____

_____

_____

_____

CHAPTER ONE

KNOWING THE VOICE OF GOD

OBJECTIVES:

Upon completion of this chapter you will be able to:

- Write the Key Verse from memory.
- Prove by Scripture that God speaks to men and women.
- Explain the relationship between knowing God's voice and determining His will.
- Distinguish between the "rhema" Word of God and the "logos" Word of God.
- Explain what is meant by the "will of God."

KEY VERSE:

My sheep hear my voice, and I know them, and they follow me. (John 10:27)

INTRODUCTION

The title of this course, "*Knowing God's Voice,*" implies several things:

First:	That there is a God.
Second:	That He communicates with man.
Third:	That man can recognize His voice when He speaks.
Fourth:	That God has something to say.

Let us examine each of these statements:

First: This course is based upon the truth that there is a God who is revealed to man through the written record of His Word, the Holy Bible.

Second: The Bible is the inspired written record of God's communication to man. It details the ways which God spoke to man and the response of individuals and nations to the voice of God. The Bible often repeats the phrase ". . . and the Lord said" and incidents where He spoke to man. This confirms that God communicates with men and women.

For an example, read the story of Balaam in Numbers chapter 22. God spoke to Balaam, but he refused to listen. God wanted to communicate to this man so much that He actually resorted to using a donkey. Balaam was:

. . . rebuked for his iniquity; the dumb ass speaking with man's voice forbad the madness of the prophet. (II Peter 2:16)

Third: The Bible verifies that believers can know the voice of God. Jesus said:

I am the good shepherd and know my sheep , and am known of mine. . .

And other sheep I have, which are not of this fold: them also I must bring, and they shall hear my voice, and there shall be one fold, and one shepherd.

My sheep hear my voice, and I know them, and they follow me. . .
(John 10:14,16,27)

Fourth: God has something important to say to mankind. We are warned:

Wherefore (as the Holy Ghost saith), Today if ye will hear His voice,
Harden not your hearts, as in the provocation, in the day of temptation in the wilderness. . .

While it is said, Today if ye will hear His voice, harden not your hearts, as in the provocation. . . (Hebrews 3:7,15)

The "temptation in the wilderness" and the "provocation" (provoking) of God mentioned in these verses refer to the disobedience of the nation of Israel.

After Israel was delivered from Egyptian captivity, they repeatedly disobeyed when God spoke to them. In these verses God warns us to respond when He speaks and not disobey as Israel did.

The phrase "today, if ye will hear His voice," confirms that God still speaks to men in present times just as He did in times past. The warning to listen confirms that what He has to say is important.

MANY VOICES

The Bible reveals that there are many voices in the world clamoring for attention:

There are, it may be, so many kinds of voices in the world, and none of them is without signification. (I Corinthians 14:10)

What are these voices in the world?

THE VOICE OF MAN:

The voice of man is easy to recognize. It is the audible voice of another human being:

Then Peter and the other apostles answered and said, We ought to obey God rather than men. (Acts 5:29)

Sometimes the voice of man may give wise advice, but anytime the voice of man conflicts with the voice of God, you must obey God.

THE VOICE OF SATAN:

The voice of Satan was first heard by man when he spoke to Eve in the Garden of Eden (Genesis 3:1,4,5). Satan's voice lies, deceives, and always attempts to lead man into sin away from God. You can easily recognize this when you read about the temptation of Jesus by Satan in Matthew 4:1-13. You can study examples of conversations Satan has with God in Job 1:7-12 and 2:1-6.

Evil spirits (demons of Satan) also have voices:

For unclean spirits, crying with loud voice, came out of many that were possessed with them. . . (Acts 8:7)

And in the synagogue there was a man, which had a spirit of an unclean devil, and cried out with a loud voice,

Saying, Let us alone; what have we to do with thee, thou Jesus of Nazareth? art thou come to destroy us? I know thee who thou art; the Holy One of God. (Luke 4:33-34)

Sometimes the voice of Satan is actually audible when demons use the vocal cords of a possessed man or woman. Most often, however, Satan speaks in an inaudible voice. He speaks lies, deceit, and sinful thoughts into your mind.

THE VOICE OF SELF:

The voice of self is man talking to himself. You can read examples of this in Luke 16:3 and 18:4 and in Jonah 4:8 where the prophet wished in himself to die. The Bible warns concerning the voice of self:

O Lord, I know that the way of man is not in himself; it is not in man that walketh to direct his steps. (Jeremiah 10:23)

THE VOICE OF GOD:

Jesus said believers could know God's voice and distinguish it from other voices:

To Him the porter openeth; and the sheep hear His voice; and He calleth His own sheep by name, and leadeth them out.

And when He putteth forth His own sheep, He goeth before them, and the sheep follow Him; for they know His voice.

And a stranger will they not follow, but will flee from Him; for they know not the voice of strangers. (John 10:3-5)

Believers are compared to sheep. It is the characteristic of sheep not to know where they are going. They must be led. Jesus said He was the shepherd or leader of the sheep. He said His sheep would know His voice and follow Him instead of the voices of man, self, or Satan.

HEARING THE VOICE OF GOD

Open your Bible to the book of Genesis and read chapters 1-3. These chapters record the creation of the world and of the first human beings, Adam and Eve. From the time of creation, God communicated His will to mankind. He gave specific instructions to Adam and Eve. They were to name the animals, tend the Garden, have companionship with each other, and reproduce to populate the earth. Most important of all, they were to maintain intimate fellowship with God. This intimate fellowship with God enabled them to know God's voice. When God spoke, He communicated His plan to them:

And the Lord God commanded the man, saying, Of every tree of the garden thou mayest freely eat;

But of the tree of the knowledge of good and evil, thou shalt not eat of it; for in the day that thou eatest thereof thou shalt surely die. (Genesis 2:16-17)

By the voice of God the will of God was revealed to Adam and Eve. They could freely eat of every tree in the garden, with the exception of the tree of the knowledge of good and evil.

Adam and Eve did not follow God's plan. They listened to the voice of Satan and ate of the forbidden tree. When they realized what they had done, they hid themselves from God:

And they heard the voice of the Lord God walking in the garden in the cool of the day; and Adam and his wife hid themselves from the presence of the Lord God amongst the trees of the garden.

And the Lord God called unto Adam, and said unto him, Where art thou? (Genesis 3:8-9)

It is sin which separates man from God. God did not remove His presence from man. Because of sin, man hid himself from the presence of God. Sin results in a hardened heart. The Bible warns:

**While it is said, Today if ye will hear His voice, harden not your hearts. . .
(Hebrews 3:15)**

God wants to communicate to man, but communication requires relationship. Sin separates man from intimate relationship to God, hardens his heart, and hinders him from knowing the voice of God.

THE VOICE AND THE WILL

Believers often ask, "What is God will for me?" What do we actually mean when we say we want to know the will of God? It means we want to know His general plan for our lives. We want His guidance in specific decisions so we can make wise choices. We desire His direction in the circumstances of life. The question we should be asking is, "How can I know the voice of God?" Knowing God's voice results in finding the will of God.

God wants you to know His will:

**Wherefore be ye not unwise, but understanding what the will of the Lord is.
(Ephesians 5:17)**

If you know His voice then you will understand His will as He speaks it to you. Learning to receive divine guidance is learning to walk in intimate fellowship with God. The Bible says:

**Man shall not live by bread alone, but by every word that proceedeth out of
the mouth of God. (Matthew 4:4)**

The word "proceedeth" speaks of a continuing function. It means something that happened in the past, is happening in the present, and will continue in the future. God speaks to communicate His will to mankind. This is why it is important to know the voice of God.

WHEN GOD SPEAKS

There are two Greek words translated as "word" in the Bible. The Greek words are "logos" and "rhema." "Logos" refers to the written Word of God. "Rhema" refers to the living or life-giving Word of God. It was said of believers in the city of Berea:

**These were more noble than those in Thessalonica, in that they received the
word (rhema) with all readiness of mind, and searched the Scriptures (logos)
daily, whether those things were so. (Acts 17:11)**

This verse illustrates the relationship of the "logos" and "rhema" word. The "logos" or written Word always agrees with the "rhema" or spoken, life-giving Word. This is how you can know the voice you hear is from the Lord. A "rhema" Word from God usually applies to a specific situation, meets a personal need, and provides individual guidance. Because you recognize the Word as applying to a specific need or situation in your life, it becomes a life-giving Word to you.

A "rhema" Word may be communicated through a sermon or a verse from the Bible which suddenly strikes you with great meaning. It may be spoken to you by God through the use of spiritual gifts. It may also be spoken in your inner spirit by the Lord. (You will learn more about how God speaks through spiritual gifts and in your spirit in later chapters.)

But remember: The "rhema" Word will always agree with the written Word of God. The written Word of God is complete. Nothing is to be added to it or taken from it (Revelation 22:18-19). When God speaks through the "rhema" Word it will always be in harmony with His written Word.

TYPES OF LISTENERS

The Bible speaks of two main divisions of listeners:

> **Therefore whosoever heareth these sayings of mine and doeth them, I will liken him unto a wise man, which built his house upon a rock. . .**
>
> **And every one that heareth these sayings of mine, and doeth them not shall be likened unto a foolish man, which built his house upon the sand. . . (Matthew 7:24,26)**

A foolish listener hears the voice of God, but does not act upon it. A wise listener hears and acts upon the message of God. One listener is a "hearer of the Word" only. The other is both a "hearer and a doer."

You must not only come to know the voice of God, you must learn to respond in obedience to that voice:

> **But be ye doers of the Word, and not hearers only, deceiving your own selves.**
>
> **For if any be a hearer of the Word, and not a doer, he is like unto a man beholding his natural face in a glass:**
>
> **For he beholdeth himself, and goeth his way, and straightway forgetteth what manner of man he was.**
>
> **But whoso looketh into the perfect law of liberty, and continueth therein, he being not a forgetful hearer, but a doer of the work, this man shall be blessed in his deed. (James 1:22-25)**

Jesus also told a story about seed sown in several types of soil which illustrates various types of listeners. Read the story in Matthew 13:1-9. Jesus explains the story in Matthew 13:18-23. He compares the different soils to listeners and their response to the Word of God.

SEED BY THE WAYSIDE:

Some seed fell by the wayside and was snatched up by birds before it could take root. This is an example of a man who hears the voice of God but the words do not take root in his heart. Satan snatches away God's Word.

SEED IN STONY PLACES:

Some seed fell in stony places and sprang up quickly. But when the heat of the sun came, the plant withered and died because it had no roots. This is the listener who hears God's Word and receives it with joy, but it does not really take root in his life. When circumstances get tough, he is offended and ceases to respond to God's voice.

SEED AMONG THE THORNS:
Some seed fell among thorns which choked outgrowth of the plants. This is an example of the voice of God being choked out by the cares of the world, materialism, etc.

SEED ON GOOD GROUND:

Some seed fell on good ground and brought forth a rich harvest. This is an example of the listener who receives God's Word, listens to His voice, and roots himself in that revelation. This person will mature spiritually and become a reproducing, fruitful believer.

HOW CAN YOU KNOW GOD'S VOICE?

Do you want to be able to know God's voice? Do you want to know His will for your life? In the next chapter you will learn of requirements which prepare you to hear the voice of God and discover His will for your life.

SELF-TEST

1. Write the Key Verse from memory:

    _____

    _____

2. What is meant by the "rhema" Word of God?

    _____

3. What is meant by the "logos" Word of God?

    _____

4. How is knowing God's voice related to determining His will for your life?

    _____

5. Give a reference from the book of Hebrews which confirms God spoke to men in the past and still speaks today.

    _____

6. What is meant by the "will of God"?

    _____

    _____

7. With what does the "rhema" Word of God always agree?

    _____

8. What separated man from God's presence?_____

9. You must be a_____of the Word and not a_____only.

(Answers to tests are provided at the conclusion of the final chapter in this manual.)

FOR FURTHER STUDY

1. There are several verses in the Bible which describe the voice of God. Look up each reference and record the words describing God's voice. The first one is done as an example for you to follow. From your own study of the Bible you can continue to add references and descriptions of the voice of God to this chart.

Reference	Description Of God's Voice
II Samuel 22:14	Thunder from Heaven
I Kings 19:12-13	
Psalms 18:13	
Psalms 29:3-9	
Psalms 68:33	
Daniel 10:6-9	

2. God spoke about Jesus. You can read what He said in the following passages: II Peter 1:17-18; Matthew 3:17; Mark 1:11

3. What God speaks comes to pass. See Ezekiel 12:25-28.

4. Study the words of Jesus in the books of Matthew, Mark, Luke, and John. Observe how Jesus spoke in questions, answers, examples, parallels, parables, and sermons.

5. God not only speaks to individuals but He also speaks to nations. See Jeremiah 18:7-10.

6. Read about the results of disobeying God's voice in the following verses. Record the results of disobedience on the chart:

Reference	Results Of Disobedience
Exodus 15:26	
Deuteronomy 28:15-68	
I Samuel 12:15	

7. Read the following Scriptures and record what you learn about the results of obeying God's voice:

Deuteronomy 28:1-14:_____

I Samuel 12:14:_____

8. The entire Bible is a record of how individuals and nations responded to the voice of God. Complete the following chart as you study the response of man to God's voice. The first one is done as an example for you to follow.   You may need to read verses before and after the reference given in order to obtain the information needed to complete the chart. Like the previous chart, you can continue to add references from your own study of God's Word.

Reference	People	Response	Results
Genesis 26:5	Abraham	Obedience	His seed and the nations of the world were blessed.
Genesis 22:18			
Deuteronomy 8:20			
Judges 2:2,4,20-23			
Judges 6:10			
I Samuel 15:1,19,22,24			
I Samuel 28:18			
Psalms 106:25			
Jeremiah 32:23			
Daniel 9:10-14			
Zephaniah 3:2			
Haggai 1:12			

CHAPTER TWO

"IF ANY MAN WILL DO. . . HE SHALL KNOW"

OBJECTIVES:

Upon completion of this chapter you will be able to:

- Write the Key Verses from memory.
- Define the word "prerequisite."
- List prerequisites for knowing the voice of God.
- Explain what it means to be born again.
- Recognize the importance of the Holy Spirit in to knowing God's voice.
- Demonstrate understanding of "spiritual maturity" and "transformation."

KEY VERSES:

> **I beseech you therefore brethren, by the mercies of God, that you present your bodies a living sacrifice, holy, acceptable unto God, which is your reasonable service.**
>
> **And be not conformed to this world; but be ye transformed by the renewing of your mind, that ye may prove what is that good, and acceptable, and perfect will of God. (Romans 12:1-2)**

INTRODUCTION

There are some necessary prerequisites if you are to come to know the voice of God. A prerequisite is something you must do before you can do something else. It is something required before you are able to reach a certain goal.

Your goal in this course is to come to know the voice of God. This chapter explains the prerequisites (the things required) before you can achieve this objective. Jesus said:

> **If any man will do His will, He shall know of the doctrine, whether it be of God, or whether I speak of myself. (John 7:17)**

The Key Verses of this chapter, Romans 12:1-2, list some things that are God's will for you to do. If you meet these prerequisites, then you will come to know God's voice and His will for your life.

BORN-AGAIN EXPERIENCE

I beseech you therefore brethren, by the mercies of God, that ye present your bodies a living sacrifice, holy, acceptable unto God, which is your reasonable service. (Romans 12:1)

As you learned in the previous chapter, sin separates you from God's presence. Because of sin, you have difficulty hearing and responding positively to the voice of God.

In the natural world you do not recognize the voice of a stranger. You recognize voices of those you know and with whom you have developed a relationship. The same is true in the spiritual world. If you are to come to know God's voice, you must first come to know God and you cannot develop an intimate relationship with Him with sin in your life.

Romans 12:1 requires that YOU make the move towards God by giving your life to Him. God has already spoken through His written Word and revealed it is His will for you to develop such a relationship:

> **The Lord is not slack concerning His promise, as some men count slackness; but is longsuffering to usward, not willing that any should perish, but that all should come to repentance. (II Peter 3:9)**

God does not want you to spend your life in sin. He wants you to live it according to His plan:

> **That he no longer should live the rest of his time in the flesh to the lusts of men, but to the will of God. (I Peter 4:2)**

God is pictured standing at the door of your life desiring entrance so He can develop a relationship with you:

> **Behold, I stand at the door, and knock: if any man hear my voice, and open the door, I will come in to him, and will sup with him, and he with me. (Revelation 3:20)**

God's stated purpose from the beginning of the world was to bring all men into the knowledge of Christ Jesus:

> **Having made known unto us the mystery of His will, according to His good pleasure which He hath purposed in Himself:**
>
> **That in the dispensation of the fulness of times He might gather together in one all things in Christ, both which are in heaven, and which are on earth; even in Him. (Ephesians 1:9-10)**

You are "gathered into Christ" by becoming part of the family of God. Just as you are born into a natural family, you must be "born again" spiritually into this spiritual family.

Read John chapter 3. This chapter explains in detail what it means to be born-again. To experience the new birth you must:

1. Acknowledge you are a sinner:

    For all have sinned and come short of the glory of God. (Romans 3:23)

2. Recognize the penalty of sin is death:

God warned Adam and Eve that if they sinned, they would die. This meant both spiritual death (separation from God's presence) and physical death. When Jesus died on the cross He died in your place. He died for your sins so you could have everlasting life:

    For the wages of sin is death, but the gift of God eternal life through Jesus Christ our Lord. (Romans 6:23)

If you accept His sacrifice for sin, you are no longer under the penalty of death.

3. Confess your sins, ask forgiveness, and believe that Jesus died for you:

    If we say that we have no sin, we deceive ourselves and the truth is not in us.

    If we confess our sins, He is faithful and just to forgive us our sins, and to cleanse us from all unrighteousness. (I John 1:8-9)

    For God so loved the world that He gave His only begotten Son that whosoever believeth in Him should not perish but have everlasting life. (John 3:16)

When you present your life to God in this manner, you are "born-again" spiritually:

    Therefore, if any man be in Christ He a new creature; old things have passed away; Behold, all things are become new. (II Corinthians 5:17)

When you are born again you become part of God's spiritual family. You are no longer separated from the presence of God. When you die physically, you will live eternally with Him.

You have established a relationship with God through Jesus Christ. You have heard and responded to the truth of the Gospel. You are now in a position to learn how to recognize God's voice:

. . . Every one that is of the truth heareth my voice. (John 18:37)

INDWELLING OF THE HOLY SPIRIT

There is another prerequisite that will help you come to know God's voice. The Bible speaks of an experience called the Baptism of the Holy Spirit. This experience results in the Holy Spirit dwelling in your life and empowering you to live a holy life which is acceptable to God.

The ministries of the Holy Spirit in the life of the believer are too numerous to discuss in this lesson. The Harvestime International Network course entitled "*The Ministry Of The Holy Spirit*" is devoted to this subject and provides instructions on how to receive the Baptism of the Holy Spirit.

One of the most important ministries of the indwelling Holy Spirit is to guide the believer into God's will:

> **When He, the Spirit of truth is come (the Holy Spirit), He will guide you into all truth. . . and He will show you things to come and He shall receive of mine (God's will) and show it to you. (John 16:13-14)**

The Bible says:

> **For as many as are led by the Spirit of God, they are the sons of God. (Romans 8:14)**

There is a definite relationship between being a child of God (born again) and being led by the Holy Spirit. The natural man (who is not born-again) does not receive and follow guidance of the Holy Spirit. Because he has not become a "spiritual man" through the new birth experience, He does not recognize the voice of God:

> **But the natural man receiveth not the things of the Spirit of God; for they are foolishness unto him; neither can he know them, because they are spiritually discerned. (I Corinthians 2:14)**

The following examples from the book of Acts demonstrate the leading of the Holy Spirit in the lives of believers:

PHILIP:

A church deacon by the name of Philip was led by the Spirit to join a chariot he saw on a desert road to Gaza:

> **Then the Spirit said unto Philip, Go near and join thyself to this chariot. (Acts 8:29)**

Philip obeyed the leading of the Holy Spirit. This resulted in the salvation and water baptism of an Ethiopian man who was riding in the chariot.

PETER:

Peter was told by the Holy Spirit to go with three men who came from Caesarea. Peter said:

And the Spirit bade me go with them, nothing doubting. (Acts 11:12)

Peter recognized the leading of the Holy Spirit. He had no doubts when the Spirit spoke in his inner being and revealed God's will to him. He obeyed and it resulted in the first cross-cultural ministry to the Gentiles.

PAUL:

Paul often changed his evangelistic schedule at the prompting of the Holy Spirit:

After they were come to Mysia, they assayed to go into Bithynia; but the Spirit suffered them not. (Acts 16:7)

Paul planned to go to Mysia, but the Holy Spirit gave him different directions.

These three examples are just a few of many in the Bible which illustrate how the Holy Spirit enables you to hear God's voice. As Jesus promised, the Holy Spirit takes the will of God and reveals it to you.

SPIRITUAL MATURITY

And be not conformed to this world. . . (Romans 12:2)

In the natural world when a baby is born he must attain a certain level of maturity before he begins to recognize the voice of his parents. The same is true in the spiritual world. When you are first born again you may not be able to recognize the voice of God when He speaks to you. When you first receive the Holy Spirit you may not always understand when the Spirit reveals God's will to you. But the Holy Spirit will continue to reveal God's will and guide you. As you mature spiritually, you will come to recognize this voice within your spirit.

The Bible speaks of this parallel between the natural and spiritual:

For every one that useth milk is unskillful in the word of righteousness: For he is a babe.

But strong meat belongeth to them that are of full age, even those who by reason of use have their senses exercised to discern both good and evil. (Hebrews 5:13-14)

The "milk" and "meat" mentioned in these verses refer to the written Word of God, the Holy Bible. When you are first born again you start learning some of the simple truths (milk) of the written Word of God. As you mature, you are able to master the deeper truths (meat) of the Word of God.

As you continue to study God's written Word, your spiritual senses will mature. You will be able to exercise them to discern good and evil. This means you will be able to distinguish God's will and His way from the wrong ways of life. This is why it is important for you to study God's written Word.

As you mature spiritually, you will no longer "conform" to the world. To be conformed means to be fashioned or shaped according to a set standard. Spiritual maturity will conform you to the image of Christ rather than the image of worldly standards.
Spiritual maturity also helps you achieve emotional maturity. If you lack emotional maturity, important decisions may be made in a fit of anger or self-pity. This can have disastrous long-range results.

As you mature spiritually you will develop the "Fruit of the Holy Spirit," evidences of spiritual maturity that result in emotional maturity:

But the fruit of the Spirit is love, joy, peace, longsuffering, gentleness, goodness, faith, Meekness, temperance: against such there is no law. (Galatians 5:22-23)

TRANSFORMATION

. . . But be ye transformed by the renewing of your mind. . . (Romans 12:2)

Spiritual maturity leads finally to transformation, another prerequisite that enables you to know the voice of God. What natural man (human nature) desires to do and what God desires for your life is different. This creates a conflict between the flesh (natural man) and the spirit (spiritual man).

Paul wrote of this conflict:

For the flesh lusteth against the Spirit, and the Spirit against the flesh; and these are contrary the one to the other; so that ye cannot do the things ye would. (Galatians 5:17)

Paul recognized there is a continuing struggle of the flesh against the Spirit in matters relating to the fulfilling of God's will. He identified this struggle as taking place in the mind:

> But I see another law in my members, warring against the law of my mind, and bringing me into captivity to the law of sin which is in my members. (Romans 7:23)

Because of this he urged:

> I beseech you therefore, brethren, by the mercies of God, that ye present your bodies a living sacrifice, holy, acceptable unto God, which is your reasonable service.
>
> And be not conformed to this world; but be ye transformed by the renewing of your mind, that ye may prove what is that good, and acceptable, and perfect will of God. (Romans 12:1-2)

The word "beseech" means to plead, implore, or beg. The phrase "present your bodies a living sacrifice" indicates an unreserved surrender to God.

To offer something for a sacrifice means to give it up completely. In the Old Testament when a sacrifice was made, it was given completely to God to be burned with fire, consumed by the priest, or both, as the law indicated. The giver of the sacrifice had no further claim to it.

So must be our surrender to God. The natural man, the old self nature must die to the world and the flesh. This is what is meant by "transformation." It is being changed into another image patterned after the Lord Jesus Christ:

> I am crucified with Christ. (Galatians 2:20)
>
> They that are Christ's have crucified the flesh. (Galatians 5:24)
>
> But I keep under my body, and bring it into subjection; lest that by any means, when I have preached to others, I myself should be a castaway. (I Corinthians 9:27)
>
> Let not sin therefore reign in your mortal body, that ye should obey it in the lusts thereof. (Romans 6:12)
>
> Having therefore these promises, dearly beloved, let us cleanse ourselves from all filthiness of the flesh and spirit, perfecting holiness in the fear of God. (II Corinthians 7:1)
>
> Likewise reckon ye also yourselves to be dead indeed unto sin. (Romans 6:11)

24

Actual physical crucifixion, as Jesus experienced, is an unnatural death. There is significance in the fact that the death prescribed for the self-nature is crucifixion. The fleshly nature of man will never die a natural death. It will not die voluntarily. It must be put to death by force just as in actual crucifixion in the natural world.

According to Romans 12:1-2, such surrender precedes the knowledge of God's will. If you want to know God's voice and His will, you must first surrender. We often want to reverse the process. We want to know His will, then decide if we will surrender to it. But Romans 12:1-2 indicates surrender comes first.

The reason we are hesitant about surrender is because we do not understand God's will is always acceptable, good, and perfect. We are afraid to surrender to God totally because we have not grasped this basic concept:

> **For I know the plans I have for you, says the Lord. They are plans for good and not for evil, to give you a future and a hope. (Jeremiah 29:11 TLB)**

RENEWING YOUR MIND

Your mind is naturally conformed to the principles of the world around you. It happens because of your basic sin nature. It also happens through the influence of your culture.

But God says you are not to conform to the world but to be transformed. The word "transform" means to be changed or into a new image. The pattern for that image is the Lord Jesus Christ:

> **But we all, with open face, beholding as in a glass the glory of the Lord, are changed into the same image from glory to glory, even as by the Spirit of the Lord. (II Corinthians 3:18)**

According to Romans 12:2, transformation comes through renewing your mind. This means you must get rid of worldly standards and principles and conform to the principles revealed in

God's written Word.

Your mind is transformed as you develop the mind of Christ:

> **Let this mind be in you which was also in Christ Jesus. (Philippians 2:5)**

The word "let" indicates that you have to make a choice in order to have the mind of Christ. You must permit the transformation of the mind to happen. You have a responsibility in development of the transformed mind. It is not something done automatically for you by God:

> **Wherefore (YOU) gird up the loins of your mind. (I Peter 1:13)**

To "gird up" the mind means to clothe or protect your mental powers. To transform or gird up the mind, it is necessary to immerse it in the Word of God. Search the Bible to discover what type of mind was in Christ. (The "For Further Study" section of this chapter will help you do this.)

Your mind is transformed as God puts His laws into it:

> **. . . I will put my laws into their mind. (Hebrews 8:10)**

Use the power of the mind to cast down and bring into captivity wrong thoughts:

> **Casting down imaginations, and every high thing that exalteth itself against the knowledge of God, and bringing into captivity every thought to the obedience of Christ. (II Corinthians 10:5)**

You have the responsibility to control your thought life:

> **Finally, brethren, whatsoever things are true, whatsoever things are honest, whatsoever things are just, whatsoever things are pure, whatsoever things are lovely, whatsoever things are of good report; if there be any virtue, and if there by any praise, think on these things. (Philippians 4:8)**

Then you can say with Paul:

> **But we have the mind of Christ. (I Corinthians 2:6)**

The mind of Christ was set and determined to do the will of God.

PROVING GOD'S WILL

Study the following chart. You will discover that each prerequisite discussed in this chapter is included in Romans 12:1-2:

I beseech you therefore brethren by the mercies of God...	You come to God through His mercy extended through the sacrifice of Jesus for your sins.
that you present your bodies a living sacrifice, holy, acceptable unto God, which is your reasonable service...	Spiritual maturity is enabled by the working of the Holy Spirit in your life.
And be not conformed to this world but be ye transformed by the renewing of your mind.	You are transformed by the Word, your mind is renewed.

The new birth experience, the indwelling of the Holy Spirit, spiritual maturity, and transformation of the mind--how do these relate to knowing God's will?   According to Romans 12:1-2 they are prerequisites leading to knowledge of His will:

> **. . . that ye may prove what is that good, and acceptable, and perfect will of God. (Romans 12:2)**

The word "prove" means to determine, confirm, and be sure of something. These prerequisites lead to assurance of the will of God.

But what exactly is meant by the "will of God"? And what are the "good, perfect, and acceptable" wills of God? Why is it important to "prove" or determine God's will?

We will explore answers to these questions in the following chapters.

SELF-TEST

1. Write the Key Verses from memory.

_____

_____

2. What does the word "prerequisite" mean?

_____

3. What are the prerequisites presented in this chapter as necessary in order to know God's will?

_____

4. What is the main ministry of the Holy Spirit as it relates to knowing God's voice?

_____

5. What does it mean to be born-again?

_____

6. Why is it necessary to be born again in order to come to know the voice of God?

_____

7. What does it mean to be spiritually mature?

_____

8. Define the word "transformed" as it was used in this chapter.

_____

9. Is this statement true or false: According to Romans 12:1-2 surrender precedes the knowledge of God's will. The statement is:_____

(Answers to tests are provided at the conclusion of the final chapter in this manual.)

FOR FURTHER STUDY

1. For further study of the new birth and spiritual maturity, obtain the Harvestime International Institute course "*Foundations Of Faith.*" For further study of the Holy Spirit, obtain the Harvestime International Institute course "*The Ministry Of The Holy Spirit.*"

2. This chapter spoke of the necessity of transformation of the mind. The Scriptures indicate believers are NOT to have minds that are:

Hardened:	Daniel 5:20
Reprobate:	Romans 1:28
Carnal:	Romans 8:6
Doubtful:	Luke 12:29
Blinded:	II Corinthians 3:14; 4:14
Corrupted:	II Corinthians 11:3
Fleshly:	Ephesians 2:3; Colossians 2:18
Vain:	Ephesians 4:17
Earthly:	Philippians 3:19
Alienated by wicked works:	Colossians 1:21
Double minded:	James 1:8; 4:8
Defiled:	Titus 1:15

3. The Bible indicates the transformed mind of believers should be:

Spiritual:	Romans 8:6
Ready:	I Peter 5:2
Pure:	II Peter 3:1
Stayed:	Isaiah 26:3
Peaceful:	Philippians 4:7
Renewed:	Ephesians 4:23
Humble:	Colossians 3:12
Sober:	Titus 2:6
Sound:	II Timothy 1:7
Loving:	Matthew 22:37
Serving:	Romans 7:25
Fully persuaded:	Romans 14:5
United:	I Peter 3:8; 4:1; Romans 15:6; I Corinthians 1:10
Honest and willing:	I Chronicles 28:9
Disciplined to work:	Nehemiah 4:6

CHAPTER THREE

THE WILL OF GOD

OBJECTIVES:

Upon completion of this chapter you will be able to:

- Write the Key Verse from memory.
- Define the word "will."
- Identify the three types of will at work in the world today.
- Explain the three meanings of God's will.
- List reasons why it is important to do God's will.
- Identify the proper motivation for doing God's will.

KEY VERSE:

> **For I came down from Heaven not to do mine own will, but the will of Him that sent me. (John 6:38)**

INTRODUCTION

This chapter identifies three types of will in operation in the world today. It defines the expression "God's will", examines the life of Jesus in relation to that will, and stresses the importance of the will of God.

THE MEANING OF "WILL"

The common meaning of the word "will" is to determine or decide on the basis of the will. The will is the power of choice. There are three types of will operating in the world today:

SELF-WILL:

This is the will of man, the basic selfish nature which desires to walk its own way. When you guide your life by self-will, you make choices on the basis of your will apart from God. The Bible warns about self-will:

> **O Lord, I know that the way of man is not in himself; it is not in man that walketh to direct his steps. (Jeremiah 10:23)**

Self-will is the operation of the fleshly nature of man:

> **But chiefly them that walk after the flesh in the lust of uncleanness, and despise government. Presumptuous are they, self-willed; they are not afraid to speak evil of dignities. (II Peter 2:10)**

The Bible records the results of self-will:

> **So I gave them up unto their own hearts' lust: and they walked in their own counsels. (Psalms 81:12)**

Sin, suffering, and trouble in the world today are all results of man living in disobedience to the will of God. David speaks of self-will operating in the lives of wicked men:

> **Deliver me not over unto the will of mine enemies: for false witnesses are risen up against me, and such as breathe out cruelty. (Psalms 27:12)**

The Bible states that leaders in the church should not be self-willed:

> **For the bishop must be blameless as the steward of God: not self willed. . . (Titus 1:7)**

SATAN'S WILL:

Satan has a will. He desires to destroy all that is good in your life. Jesus warned Peter about this:

> **And the Lord said, Simon, Simon, behold, Satan hath desired to have you, that he may sift you as wheat. (Luke 22:31)**

Satan wants to sift all that is good out of your life. Jesus said:

> **The thief cometh not, but for to steal, and to kill, and to destroy: I am come that they might have life, and that they might have it more abundantly. (John 10:10)**

Paul said some believers are taken captive by the will of Satan:

> **And that they may recover themselves out of the snare of the devil, who are taken captive by him at his will. (II Timothy 2:26)**

GOD'S WILL:

The third will operating in the world is the will of God. This is the subject of our study.

THE MEANING OF GOD'S WILL

The New Testament was originally written in the Greek language. In Greek there are two terms used for the word "will" in reference to the will of God.

One word is "boulema," which refers to God's sovereign will. This is His predetermined plan for everything that happens in the universe. This type of "God's will" is fulfilled regardless of decisions made by man. It is His master plan for the world.

The "boulema" will of God does not require the cooperation of man. In the "boulema" will of God, the outcome is predetermined. The "boulema" will of God is written in His Word and is quite clear. There is no need to seek this will of God because it is revealed in the Bible.

The other word "thelema" refers to God's desire for man to experience and live in His will. It refers to His individual plan or will for each man and women. In order for God to fulfill His "thelema" will, it requires your cooperation. You have the power to choose whether or not you will walk in the "thelema" or individual will of God for your life. It is this "thelema" will, or God's will for you as an individual, to which we refer when we speak of seeking God's will.

One other type of God's will is the "moral" will of God, commandments revealed in the written Word of God which teach how believers should live. The individual and sovereign wills of God for man never conflict with the moral will of God as revealed in His Word. The following chart summarizes the various meanings of the "will of God":

Sovereign (Boulema)	Individual (Thelema)	Moral
God's predetermined plan for the universe	God's detailed plan for each individual	The moral commands revealed it the written Word of God which teach how we should believe and live
Unaffected by the decisions of man	Affected by the decisions of man	The individual will of God in harmony with His moral will

JESUS AND GOD'S WILL

God's will was the chief concern of Jesus during His earthly ministry. He declared:

> **For I came down from Heaven, not to do mine own will, but the will of Him that sent me. (John 6:39)**

God's will was to bring men and women into right relationship with Him:

> **And this is the Father's will which hath sent me, that of all which He hath given me I should lose nothing, but should raise it up again at the last day. (John 6:38)**

> **And this is the will of Him that sent me, that every one which seeth the Son, and believeth on Him, may have everlasting life; and I will raise him up at the last day. (John 6:40)**

The purpose of Christ's life was to fulfill God's will. Even as a child, Jesus was concerned with doing God's will. When He was in the temple and His parents came looking for Him, Jesus said:

> **Wist ye not that I must be about my Father's business? (Luke 2:49)**

The secret of His spiritual strength was found in doing God's will:

> **Jesus saith unto them, My meat is to do the will of Him that sent me, and to finish His work. (John 4:34)**

This verse reveals His concern with finishing God's work through His life and ministry.

The power evident in Christ's earthly ministry is related to the will of God:

> **I can of mine own self do nothing; as I hear, I judge; and my judgment is just; because I seek not mine own will, but the will of the Father which hath sent me. (John 5:30)**

Christ's words and deeds were not His own. He spoke and acted according to the Father's will:

> **My doctrine is not mine, but His that sent me. (John 7:16)**
> **The word which ye hear is not mine, but the Father's. (John 14:24)**
> **I do nothing of myself, but as my Father has taught me. (John 8:28)**
> **I seek not my own will, but the will of the Father which hath sent me. (John 5:30)**

Even as He faced death by crucifixion, Jesus prayed:

> **. . . O my Father, if it be possible let this cup pass from me: nevertheless, not as I will, but as thou wilt. (Matthew 26:39)**

Jesus was willing to die if it was God's will for Him to do so. The life of Jesus is a perfect example of absolute conformity to the sovereign, moral, and individual will of God.

THE IMPORTANCE OF GOD'S WILL

God's will is important because. . .

IT DETERMINES YOUR ETERNAL DESTINY:

Your eternal destiny depends on doing God's will. You must respond positively to God's plan of redemption for your life. . .

> **Because straight is the gate and narrow is the way, which leadeth unto life, and few there be that find it. (Matthew 7:14)**
>
> **Not every one that saith unto me, Lord, Lord, shall enter into the Kingdom of Heaven; but he that doeth the will of My Father which is in Heaven. (Matthew 7:21)**
>
> **And the world passeth away, and the lust thereof: but he that doeth the will of God abideth forever. (I John 2:17)**

IT IS THE BASIS OF YOUR RELATIONSHIP WITH GOD:

Your relationship to Jesus is based on doing His will:

> **For whosoever shall do the will of God, the same is my brother, and my sister, and mother. (Mark 3:35 See also Matthew 12:50)**

IT PROVIDES DIRECTION:

God's will is important because you are incapable of directing your own way:

> **O Lord, I know that the way of man is not in himself; it is not in man that walketh to direct his steps. (Jeremiah 10:23)**

You lack the ability to guide your own steps. Without God's guidance you go your own way and stray from the plan of God:

All we like sheep have gone astray; we have turned everyone to his own way. (Isaiah 53:6)

IT PROVIDES KNOWLEDGE OF THE FUTURE:

God is the only one with knowledge of the future. He knows the snares of Satan that await you. He knows the future of the economic and political systems. He knows what events await you in the future:

I am God, and there is none like me, declaring the end from the beginning, and from ancient times the things that are not yet done. (Isaiah 46:9-10)

Man is able to function in the present and recall the past. He can also plan for the future. But God is the only one with actual knowledge of the future.

Some people think Satan has foreknowledge of the future. He does not. If he did, he never would have motivated the crucifixion of Jesus. He would have been able to look into the future and see that by this act redemption from sin would become a reality. Satan only knows what God chooses to reveal about the future. For example, Satan knows that his eternal destiny is Hell because God revealed it.

IT IS COMMANDED THAT YOU KNOW IT:

Knowing God's will is also important because you are commanded to know and do it:

Wherefore be ye not unwise, but understanding what the will of the Lord is. (Ephesians 5:17)

As the servant of Christ, doing the will of God from the heart. (Ephesians 6:6)

God desires your obedience to His will more than He desires your sacrifices or praise:

And Samuel said, Hath the Lord as great delight in burnt offerings and sacrifices as in obeying the voice of the Lord? Behold, to obey is better than sacrifice, and to hearken than the fat of rams.

For rebellion is as the sin of witchcraft, and stubbornness as iniquity and idolatry. . . (I Samuel 15:22-23)

God wants you to stand perfect and complete in His will:

Epaphras, who is one of you, a servant of Christ, saluteth you, always labouring fervently for you in prayers, that ye may stand perfect and

complete in all the will of God. (Colossians 4:12)

IT RESULTS IN DOCTRINAL SOUNDNESS:

Jesus said:

> **If any man will do His will, he shall know of the doctrine, whether it be of God, or whether I speak of myself.   (John 7:17)**

If you do God's will as it is revealed to you, then you will develop spiritual maturity in judging sound doctrine. This will prevent you from being deceived by false teaching.

IT RESULTS IN ANSWERED PRAYER:

When you are living in the will of God you can pray with confidence that your requests will be answered:

> **And whatsoever we ask, we receive of Him because we keep His commandments, and do those things that are pleasing in His sight. (I John 3:22)**

> **Now we know that God heareth not sinners; but if any man be a worshiper of God, and doeth His will, him He heareth. (John 9:31)**

> **And this is the confidence that we have in Him, that, if we ask anything according to His will, He heareth us. (I John 5:14)**

IT BRINGS SPIRITUAL BLESSINGS:

Spiritual blessings are promised if you do God's will:

> **For ye have need of patience, that, after ye have done the will of God, ye might receive the promise. (Hebrews 10:36)**

Blessings will actually pursue you:

> **And it shall come to pass, if thou shalt hearken diligently unto the voice of the Lord thy God, to serve and to do all His commandments which I command thee this day, that the Lord thy God will set thee on high above all nations of the earth;**

> **And all these blessing shall come on thee, and overtake thee, if thou shalt hearken unto the voice of the Lord thy God. (Deuteronomy 28:1-2)**

IT HELPS YOU AVOID CHASTISEMENT:

Chastisement means discipline, reproof, and correction. Those who deliberately turn away from God's revealed will are chastised:

> **But it shall come to pass, if thou wilt not hearken unto the voice of the Lord thy God, to observe to do all His commandments and His statutes which I command thee this day; that all these curses shall come upon thee, and overtake thee.   (Deuteronomy 28:15)**

> **And ye have forgotten the exhortation which speaketh unto you as unto children, My son, despise not thou the chastening of the Lord,   nor faint when thou art rebuked of Him;**

> **For whom the Lord loveth, He chasteneth and scourgeth every son whom He receiveth.**

> **If ye endure chastening, God dealeth with you as with sons; for what son is he whom the father chasteneth not?**

> **But if ye are without chastisement, whereof all are partakers, then are ye bastards, and not sons.**

> **Furthermore we have had fathers of our flesh which corrected us, and we gave them reverence: shall we not much rather be in subjection unto the Father of spirits, and live?   (Hebrews 12:5-9)**

Jesus also warned:

> **And that servant, which knew his lord's will, and prepared not himself, neither did according to his will, shall be beaten with many stripes. (Luke 12:47)**

Knowing God's will is a serious matter for those who desire to live the abundant life and avoid chastisement.

IT RESULTS IN SUCCESS:

One of the instructions given to Joshua when he assumed leadership of the nation of Israel was to keep the commandments of God and walk in His ways. If he did this, Joshua had this guarantee:

> **Then thou shalt make thy way prosperous and then thou shalt have good success. (Joshua 1:8)**

Psalms also records that a man walking in God's way will be successful and "whatsoever he doeth shall prosper" (Psalms 1:3). In a world filled with failure and defeat, knowing and doing the will of God is the secret to successful living.

THE PROPER MOTIVATION

You should be motivated to do God's will because you love Him. Love desires to please the object of that love:

If ye love me, keep my commandments. (John 14:15)

He that hath my commandments and keepeth them, he it is that loveth me;

and he that loveth me shall be loved of my Father, and I will love him, and will manifest myself to him. (John 14:21)

Jesus answered and said unto him, If a man love me, he will keep my words: and my Father will love him and we will come unto him, and make our abode with him. (John 14:23)

SELF-TEST

1.   Write the Key Verse from memory.

_____

2.   What is the right motivation for doing the will of God?

_____

3.   List 10 reasons why it is important to do God's will:

_____   _____   _____   _____   _____

_____   _____   _____   _____   _____

4.   Define the word "will." _____

5.   Identify the three meanings of God's will:

_____

6.   What are the three types of will at work in the world today?

_____

7.   Read the following statements. If the statement is true, write the letter T on the blank in front of it. If the statement is false, write the letter F on the blank in front of it:

   a._____Jesus was not concerned about doing God's will.
   b._____The Bible indicates that man lacks the capacity to guide his own way correctly.
   c._____The individual will of God may sometimes disagree with the moral will of God.
   d._____Only God has complete knowledge of the future.
   e._____You can experience great spiritual blessings by walking in your own self-will.

(Answers to tests are provided at the conclusion of the final chapter in this manual.)

FOR FURTHER STUDY

1. The Apostle Paul placed great emphasis on the will of God. Study the following verses:

    Acts 16:6-10; Romans 1:10; 15:32; I Corinthians 1:1; 4:19; 16:7;
    II Corinthians 1:1; Ephesians 1:1; Colossians 1:1; II Timothy 1:1

2. The chart given in this chapter on "Three Meanings Of The Will Of God" is expanded below with the addition of Biblical references. Study these verses for further understanding of the sovereign, individual, and moral will of God.

THREE MEANINGS OF "THE WILL OF GOD"

Sovereign (Boulema)	Individual (Thelema)	Moral
God's pre-determined plan for the universe	God's detailed plan for each individual	The moral commands revealed in the written Word of God which teach how we should believe and live
Unaffected by the decisions of man	Affected by the decisions of man	The individual will of God is always in harmony with His moral will
Romans 11:33-36 Acts 2:23 Acts 4:27-28 Romans 9:19 Proverbs 16:33 Ephesians 1:11 Revelation 4:11 Proverbs 21:1 Daniel 4:35	Genesis 24 Proverbs 16:9 Psalms 32:8 Proverbs 3:5-6 Ephesians 5:17 Ephesians 6:6 Romans 12:2 Colossians 1:9 Colossians 4:12	Examples: II Corinthians 6:14 Romans 2:18 I Thessalonians 5:18 I Thessalonians 4:3 (Plus all other commands in the written Word of God)

CHAPTER FOUR

HEADING THE WRONG DIRECTION

OBJECTIVES:

Upon completion of this chapter you will be able to:

- Write the Key Verse from memory.
- Identify non-Biblical methods of seeking guidance.
- Distinguish between false and true prophets of God.
- Define the word "emulations."

KEY VERSE:

> **O Lord, I know that the way of man is not in himself: It is not in man that walketh to direct his steps. (Jeremiah 10:23)**

INTRODUCTION

It is just as important to know how not to do something as it is to know how to do it.

A great inventor in the United States named Thomas Edison conducted over 1,000 experiments which failed before he perfected the light bulb. When asked if he regretted all that wasted time, he said "No. I discovered over 1,000 ways NOT to do it." In the future, he did not have to waste time using methods which did not work.

In the Bible God warns of ways you should NOT seek guidance for your life. If you heed these warnings, you will not waste time with non-Biblical methods of guidance of which God does not approve. This will prevent you from making bad decisions and heading the wrong direction in life.

In other chapters you will learn how God revealed His will in the past and how He speaks to men in present times. But first, we must eliminate the negatives. These are the ways you should NOT seek guidance.

THE OCCULT

There are numerous Satanic practices grouped under the heading of the occult. Many of these practices are used to determine guidance. Occult practices vary from nation to nation but they include such methods as witches, shamen, sorcerers, magicians, fortune tellers, astrology, horoscopes, the reading of tea leaves, crystals, cards, and the palm of the hand. Occult practices include any form of supernatural involvement which is not of God. Such practices are motivated by Satan.

God warned His people not to deal with occult practices. You can read these warnings in Deuteronomy 18:9-14 and Exodus 22:18.

Witchcraft is the practice of witches including white and black magic, sorcery, astrology, voodoo, use of potions, spells, enchantments, and drugs. It includes all similar Satanic practices and worship. Witchcraft and other such Satanic practices are spiritual rebellion against God:

> **For rebellion is as the sin of witchcraft. . . (I Samuel 15:23)**

The Bible records that sorcerers tried to turn people away from the Gospel:

> **But Elymas the sorcerer . . . withstood them, seeking to turn away the deputy from the faith. (Acts 13:8)**

Witchcraft deceives people:

> **. . . for by thy sorceries were all nations deceived. (Revelation 18:23)**

Sorcerers will not enter the Kingdom of Heaven:

> **For without are. . . sorcerers. . . (Revelation 22:15)**

The book of Revelation reveals the end of those who use such Satanic practices:

> **But. . . sorcerers. . . shall have their part in the lake which burneth with fire and brimstone. . . (Revelation 21:8)**

No true child of God should be involved in any way with occult practices for purposes of guidance or any other reason.

METHODS OF CHANCE

Casting lots was one method of seeking guidance used in the Old Testament. You can read about the use of this method in Leviticus 16:7-10; Numbers 26:55; 27:21; and Joshua 18:10.

The casting of lots was a method of chance. The belief was that God controlled the outcome of the lot which was cast. Casting of lots was similar to the rolling of dice or flipping of a coin today.

This method of seeking guidance from God was acceptable in the Old Testament. The only New

Testament use of casting of lots by believers was prior to the coming of the Holy Spirit. The Apostles of Jesus were seeking to fill the vacancy left by Judas who had betrayed Jesus and later committed suicide. Two candidates were nominated for the position:

And they gave forth their lots; and the lot fell upon Matthias; and he was numbered with the eleven apostles. (Acts 1:26)

Matthias, the man picked to replace Judas, is never again mentioned in the New Testament record. It is the Apostle Paul who actually fills the vacancy among the Apostles. Matthias was man's choice by casting lots. The Apostle Paul was God's choice by the Holy Spirit.

After the coming of the Holy Spirit (recorded in Acts chapter 2) casting of lots was not used by believers as a means of determining direction. The guidance of the Holy Spirit replaced this Old Testament method. You should not use any method of chance to determine God's will. You must know God's voice and be led by the Holy Spirit.

FLEECES

There is one Old Testament record of the use of something called a "fleece" to determine God's will. You can read the story of Gideon's fleece in Judges 6:36-40.

God spoke to Gideon and revealed His will. To confirm what God said, Gideon put out a fleece of skin on the ground. One day he asked God to let the dew fall all around but not on the fleece. On another day He asked God for dew on the fleece and for the surrounding ground to remain dry.

There is no verse in the Bible that instructs believers to do as Gideon did during this terrible national crisis when great responsibility rested upon him. This event occurred only once in the Bible and, as casting of lots, was used only before the New Testament outpouring of the Holy Spirit.

We are not to seek God's will by putting out a fleece. Modern putting out of a fleece is usually done by saying, "If a certain thing happens, then I will know it is God's will"--but our fleeces are often things that could occur naturally.

In the one case of a "fleece" recorded in the Bible, Gideon already knew God's will. He had heard the voice of God. The fleece was used as confirmation, not for direction. It was also something that could be answered only by supernatural means.

In New Testament days when Zacharias asked for a sign to confirm God's message about the birth of John the Baptism, he was stricken dumb. This was because he did not believe the voice of God and sought a sign (Luke 1:18-20).

Jesus said that "an evil and adulterous generation seeketh after a sign" (Matthew 12:39). A fleece can be a sign of unbelief or unwillingness to do God's revealed will. Fleeces which can be answered through natural means can be deceptive and misleading.

On occasion, God has graciously answered those who have asked for some indication of what they should do by a fleece or sign. This practice, however, has been the exception rather than the rule for seeking guidance in the lives of great saints of God. Remember. . . God wants men of faith, not of fleeces. He wants men and women who know His voice when He speaks and have no need to test it by confirming signs.

FALSE PROPHETS

The Bible records the stories of many prophets of God. It reveals that God sets leaders in the church known as prophets, and explains the spiritual gift of the Holy Spirit known as prophecy (Ephesians 4:11 and I Corinthians 12:10).

To "prophesy" is to speak under the special inspiration of God. It is a special ability to receive and communicate an immediate message of God to His people through a divinely-anointed utterance. The words spoken by a prophet under divine inspiration are called prophecies. To prophesy means to declare openly words from God that exhort, edify, and comfort:

But he that prophesieth speaketh unto men to edification and exhortation, and comfort. (I Corinthians 14:3)

Prophecy never replaces the written Word of God. The Bible says prophecy will cease, but the Word of God abides forever (I Corinthians 13:8 and I Peter 1:25).

In the Old Testament people went to prophets for guidance because the gift of the Holy Spirit infilling was not yet given. It is no longer necessary to go to a prophet to receive spiritual guidance. This is one of the functions of the Holy Spirit in the life of the believer. Each believer should learn to be led by God's Spirit.

The New Testament gives no record of believers seeking guidance from prophets after the gift of the Holy Spirit was given, but God still uses this gift to confirm the future. You can study such an example in Acts 21:1-14. Agabus gave Paul a personal prophecy, in that it was given specifically to Paul.

Paul already knew what awaited him in Jerusalem. The prophecy only confirmed what would happen there. It was not a prophecy of guidance telling Paul whether or not to go to Jerusalem.

The Bible warns of false prophets in the world (Matthew 24:11, 24: Mark 13:22). Because of this, God has provided ways to identify true prophecies. The Bible states:

Having then gifts differing according to the grace that is given to us, whether prophecy, let us prophesy according to the proportion of faith. (Romans 12:6)

The phrase "in proportion to faith" means in right relation to the faith. The way to recognize true prophecies is by whether or not they are in harmony with the Bible. The Bible states:

Let the prophets speak, two or three, and let the other judge. (I Corinthians 14:29)

We are told to judge prophecies. The standard for judgment is the Word of God.

God has provided many ways to recognize false prophets. False prophets are known because what they speak does not come to pass:

But the prophet, which shall presume to speak a word in my name, which I have not commanded him to speak, or that shall speak in the name of other gods, even that prophet shall die.

And if thou say in thine heart, How shall we know the word which the Lord hath not spoken?

When a prophet speaketh in the name of the Lord, the thing follow not, nor come to pass, that is the thing which the Lord hath not spoken, but the prophet hath spoken it presumptuously: thou shalt not be afraid of him. (Deuteronomy 18:20-22)

Study the following references in your Bible which explain other ways to recognize false prophets:

-False prophets do not confess the deity of Jesus Christ: I John 4:1-3

-False prophets teach false doctrine: II Peter 2:1-3

-False prophets lead people away from obedience to God's Word: Deuteronomy 13:1-5

-False prophets deceive people with miraculous signs: Matthew 24:11-24

-False prophets make false claims: Matthew 24:23-24

-Their fruit reveals their error: One of the best ways to distinguish false prophets from true prophets is to observe their lives. The Bible says that by their "fruits" you will know them. False prophets do not have evidence of spiritual fruit in their lives: Matthew 7:16

Because there are false prophets in the world, you must exercise caution in accepting prophecies. Prophecy often has been misused to direct and control believers. When personal prophecy is given it should be examined in relation to the Scriptures and it should agree with the written Word of God. In regards to guidance, prophecy should be confirming, not directing or controlling.

Because of misuse of this spiritual gift some believers reject it totally. They will not accept the miraculous gift of prophetic utterance.   But you should not reject the ministry of the Holy Spirit because you witness a few carnal examples in a human vessel.

WRONG COUNSEL

No man can determine God's will for someone else except in matters specifically revealed in the Bible. For example, we know it is God's will that all men come to repentance, for this is taught in Scripture.

Spiritual counseling by Godly leaders has a definite place in the guidance of a believer, but no counselor has the right to control another person or determine God's will for him in matters not dealt with in the Scriptures.

When the Apostle Paul was determined to go to Jerusalem, his friends at Caesarea tried to prevent him from doing so. They warned of the serious trouble which might befall him there. When Paul rejected their counsel and went on to Jerusalem, they accepted his decision stating:

The will of the Lord be done. (Acts 21:14)

They realized that even though it was their personal desire that he should not go, Paul must determine God's will for himself.

It is important that you come to know God's voice for yourself. You cannot trust others to guide your life because there are evil spirits in the world whose intent is to deceive. We are warned:

Beloved, believe not every spirit, but try the spirits whether they are of God. (I John 4:1)

When you receive counsel from another person, that guidance should be tested against other methods of determining God's will which will be detailed in a later chapter of this study.

EMULATIONS

Emulation is listed as one of the works of the flesh in Galatians 5:20. The works of the flesh are various sinful conducts which are not pleasing to God.

Emulation is the desire to copy others and to equal or excel them. It stems from a spirit of rivalry and is a form of jealousy. Some believers emulate the successful ministries of others instead of seeking God's plan for their own lives. No two believers have the same work to do. The Holy Spirit calls people into specific ministries:

> **As they ministered to the Lord, and fasted, the Holy Ghost said, separate me Barnabas and Saul for the work whereunto I have called them.**
> **(Acts 13:2)**

The Bible states that believers have differing spiritual gifts:

> **There are diversities of gifts..but all these worketh that one and selfsame Spirit, dividing to every man severally as He will. (I Corinthians 12:4,11)**

Although we are told to "covet earnestly the best gifts" (I Corinthians 12:31) and to "desire spiritual gifts" (I Corinthians 14:1), it does not mean we are to imitate others who have significant ministries. When Peter was concerned about John's ministry, Jesus said:

> **What is that to thee? Follow thou me. (John 21:22)**

God gave Noah the plan for an ark. He gave Moses the plan for the tabernacle. He gave Solomon the plan for a great temple of worship. Nehemiah was given the plan to rebuild the walls of Jerusalem. God has not told you to build an ark, construct the temple, or build walls around the city of Jerusalem. But God has a special plan for you! If you fall into the sin of emulations and imitate others, you will miss His plan.

When you pattern your life after the lives of others, you become engulfed by human tradition--and human tradition conceals divine revelation.

SELF-TEST

1. Write the Key Verse from memory.

    _____

    _____

2. What does the word "emulations" mean?

    _____

3. Read the statements below. If the statement is TRUE put the letter T in the blank provided in front of it. If the statement is FALSE write the letter F in the blank in front of it:

    a._____The Bible teaches it is acceptable to seek guidance through occult practices.

    b._____If you cannot get guidance for yourself from God, it is safe to depend on other people to guide your life.

    c._____You should always accept what a prophet says to you as truth and God's will for your life.

    d._____Human tradition conceals divine revelation.

    e._____"Casting of lots" and other methods of chance are good ways to determine God's will.

    f._____The Bible teaches putting out a fleece is one sure way to determine God's will.

    g._____One of the best ways to distinguish false from true prophets is to observe their conduct.

    h._____True prophecy always agrees with the written Word of God.

    i._____Personal prophecy should be for confirmation only, not direction or guidance.

    (Answers to tests are provided at the conclusion of the final chapter in this manual.)

FOR FURTHER STUDY

The Bible records the stories of great men of God who headed the wrong direction because they did not listen to the voice of God. Read and summarize what you learn about. . .

King Saul who went to a witch for guidance: I Samuel 28.

_____

_____

_____

Manasseh who consulted sorcerer: II Chronicles 33:16.

_____

_____

_____

An unnamed man of God who listened to a man who claimed to be a prophet instead of obeying what God told him to do: I Kings 13.

_____

_____

_____

Balaam who listened to wrong counsel of man: Numbers 22.

_____

_____

_____

CHAPTER FIVE

THE PATTERN OF GOD'S WILL

OBJECTIVES:

Upon completion of this chapter you will be able to:

- Write the Key Verses from memory.
- List basic facts concerning the will of God.
- Identify two major divisions of God's will.
- Use God's written Word to make decisions in life situations.
- Explain the pattern of God's will.
- Identify an illustration of the believer's developing conformity to God's will.
- Do further study of the revealed will of God in the written Word.

KEY VERSES:

> **Having made known unto us the mystery of His will, according to the good pleasure which He hath purposed in Himself;**
>
> **That in the dispensation of the fullness of times He might gather together in one all things in Christ, both which are in heaven, and which are on earth; even in Him;**
>
> **In whom also we have obtained an inheritance, being predestinated according to the purpose of Him who worketh all things after the counsel of His own will. (Ephesians 1:9-11)**

INTRODUCTION

Before you examine the methods God uses to speak to man to reveal His will, you must have some basic knowledge about the will of God. Previous chapters defined what is meant by "the will of God" and identified ways of seeking guidance which are wrong.

This chapter presents basic facts about the will of God, explains two major divisions of that will, examines the pattern of God's will, and discusses the believer's development in knowing the voice of God.

FACTS ABOUT GOD'S WILL

Here are some basic facts about God's will:

GOD WANTS YOU TO KNOW HIS WILL:

Faith that it is possible to know God's voice rests on two foundational facts:

First: The belief that God has a plan for you.
Second: The ability of God to communicate to you.

The following two chapters explain methods by which God communicates with man. As we mentioned in a previous lesson, God wants to communicate to man so much that He actually used a donkey to speak to a prophet on one occasion (Numbers 22).

The Bible commands:

Wherefore be ye not unwise, but understanding what the will of the Lord is. (Ephesians 5:17)

Paul wrote the Colossians:

For this cause we also, since the day we heard it, do not cease to pray for you, and to desire that ye might be filled with the knowledge of His will in all wisdom and spiritual understanding. (Colossians 1:9)

In Acts Paul spoke to one man and said:

. . . The God of our fathers hath chosen thee, that thou shouldest know His will, and see that Just one, and shouldest hear the voice of His mouth. (Acts 22:14)

In addition to these verses, God has given many promises of guidance in His written Word. (You will study some of these later). On the basis of these Scriptures it can be concluded that God wants you to know His will.

GOD'S WILL IS PLANNED:

God is working in this world to bring to pass all things on the basis of His plan:

In whom also we have obtained an inheritance, being predestinated according to the purpose of Him who worketh all things after the counsel of His own will. (Ephesians 1:11)

God has an overall plan for the universe which He is working out. We call this His master plan. He also has an individual plan for each person. Those plans fall within this sovereign plan and His moral will.

GOD'S PLAN IS INDIVIDUAL AND PERSONAL:

God's will for each individual includes His sovereign plan of redemption:

> **The Lord is not slack concerning His promise, as some men count slackness; but is longsuffering to usward, not willing that any should perish, but that all should come to repentance. (II Peter 3:9)**

But God's plan goes beyond the revelation of His sovereign and moral wills. God has an individual plan for each person which He seeks to communicate. The Bible confirms this by many stories of God at work in the lives of individuals. He placed men in specific situations at exact times for special purposes. Each of the life stories recorded in the Bible is unique.

God told the Prophet Jeremiah:

> **Before I formed thee in the belly I knew thee; and before thou camest out of the womb, I sanctified thee and ordained thee. (Jeremiah 1:5)**

What greater witness is there to the personal plan of God for an individual?

When the Apostle Peter was overly concerned about what ministry John was to have, Jesus said to him. . .

> **. . . If I will that he tarry till I come, what is that to thee? follow thou me. (John 21:22)**

Jesus had different plans for the lives of Peter and John.

Everywhere we look in the universe intelligent planning is apparent. The arrangement of planets, the stars, and the individual designs of each snowflake and flower reflect this planning. Given this evidence, we must conclude that the divine Creator also has an individual plan for man, the highest of His created beings.

God promised:

> **I will instruct thee and teach thee in the way which thou shalt go: I will guide thee with mine eye. (Psalms 32:8)**

An individual pathway is indicated in this verse.

Psalms 37 states that every step of a righteous man is ordered by the Lord:

> **The steps of a good man are ordered by the Lord: and he delighteth in his way. (Psalms 37:23)**

The same word used here for "ordered" is used in Psalms 8:3 in relation to the moon and stars which God created. The science of astronomy has recorded the amazing precision of the movement of heavenly bodies.

The same precision that has scheduled the movement of the planets orders the steps of believers. He promised:

> **Thine ear shall hear a word behind thee, saying This is the way, walk ye in it, when ye turn to the right hand and when ye turn to the left. (Isaiah 30:21)**

God orders not just the big events of life, but each step.

GOD'S WILL IS NOT MAN'S WAY:

God's will is often contrary to the ways of man:

> **For my thoughts are not your thoughts, neither are your ways my ways, saith the Lord.**

> **For as the heavens are higher than the earth, so are my ways higher than your ways, and my thoughts than your thoughts. (Isaiah 55:8-9)**

God's will is not always the path you would naturally select. This is why it is important to recognize the voice of God. But this does not mean the will of God is something which will bring unhappiness, as the next point reveals.

GOD'S WILL IS GOOD:

The Bible teaches that God's will is always good. Although His way may not be the one you would select, God knows what is best. Psalms 37:23 states you will delight in the way ordered by the Lord.

Paul confirms God's will is good:

> **And be not conformed to this world; but be ye transformed by the renewing of your mind that ye may prove what is that good, and acceptable, and perfect will of God. (Romans 12:2)**

GOD'S PLAN IS PROGRESSIVE:

Ephesians 2:10 states "we are His workmanship." The word "are" is the present tense. God is constantly working in your life. It is a continuing, progressive process of revealing His will.

> **For it is God which worketh in you both to will and to do of His good pleasure. (Philippians 2:13)**

Paul wrote to the Hebrew believers that it was God's desire to. . .

> **Make you perfect in every good work to do His will, working in you that which is well pleasing in His sight, through Jesus Christ: to whom be glory for ever and ever. (Hebrews 13:21)**

"Working" is in the present tense. God is continually guiding, developing, and speaking to you regarding His plan. You are promised continual guidance:

> **The Lord shall guide thee continually. (Isaiah 58:11)**

TWO DIVISIONS OF GOD'S WILL

When we speak of knowing God's voice, we must understand there are two basic divisions of the will of God. Each division is in harmony with the other:

FIRST: THAT REVEALED IN HIS WRITTEN WORD:

The first division of the will of God is that which is specifically revealed in the Bible. In a previous chapter we discussed the three meanings of "the will of God." We learned there is a sovereign, individual, and moral will of God. These are shown on the following diagram.

God's Sovereign Will

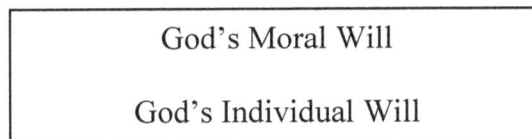

God's Moral Will
God's Individual Will

As the diagram shows, the will of God for each individual always falls within His sovereign and moral will as revealed in His written Word. The written Word of God includes the complete revelation of God's moral will. This includes all the commandments as to how you should live. As you can see on the diagram, God's sovereign will includes His moral will. It is His sovereign will that each man and woman live within the moral standards of His written Word. The written

Word of God includes portions of His sovereign will which He has chosen to reveal to us and includes the general outline of His master plan for the world and man in general.

The best summary of this plan is the Key Verses for this chapter:

> **Having made known unto us the mystery of His will, according to the good pleasure which He hath purposed in Himself;**
>
> **That in the dispensation of the fullness of times He might gather together in one all things in Christ, both which are in heaven, and which are on earth; even in Him;**
>
> **In whom also we have obtained an inheritance, being predestinated according to the purpose of Him who worketh all things after the counsel of His own will. (Ephesians 1:9-11)**

In the "For Further Study" section of this chapter we have listed specific references which are examples of God's will as revealed in His written Word.

SECOND: THAT NOT REVEALED IN HIS WORD:

The second division of God's will is that which is not revealed in His Word. This includes the individual life plan for each believer. God's Word does not reveal your specific life ministry or occupation, what church you are to attend, who you are to marry, where you are to live, etc. Yet each of these decisions are important. It is for decisions like these that you must seek God's will and be able to hear His voice when He speaks to you.

THE TWO COMPARED:

When desiring to know God's will in regards to a certain life situation, first study the Scriptures to see if specific guidance is given in the written Word of God. There is no need to "seek God's will" or ask for confirmation of His will when He has already spoken in His written Word. Examine the Scriptures carefully for specific guidance already given. Accept the written Word as God's voice speaking to you. If you refuse the guidance God has given in His written Word, you open yourself up to deception.

In many situations the Bible provides general principles--which when understood and applied-- will lead to a decision consistent with God's will. These principles apply to a variety of specific situations. For example, Paul warns:

> **Be ye not unequally yoked together with unbelievers: for what fellowship hath righteousness with unrighteousness? and what communion hath light with darkness?**

And what concord hath Christ with Belial (Satan)? or what part hath he that believeth with an infidel? (II Corinthians 6:14-15)

Here the Bible gives a general principle that believers and unbelievers should not be yoked together. This principle can be applied to many life situations: Being married to an unbeliever, going into business partnership with an unbeliever, making unbelievers your closest friends, etc.

Search the Scriptures for biographical examples which apply to your situation. Study the lives of Biblical characters to see what decisions they made in similar situations and if such decisions were in harmony with the will of God.

In matters where guidance is not given in the written Word of God, the Lord has other methods by which He speaks to man. We will examine these in the following two chapters. But remember: Guidance for individual life situations always will agree with the written Word of God. God's voice leads within the limits of the written Word. The following chart summarizes the two divisions of God's will just discussed:

TWO DIVISIONS OF GOD'S WILL	
That Revealed (Written Word)	**That Not Revealed**
Moral and sovereign will revealed in His written Word.	The individual life plan for each believer.
Includes His general will for all mankind and His master plan for the world.	Includes specific decisions such as life work, ministry, residence, education, marriage, and guidance in other specific situations.
Includes specific commandments and promises to govern living.	
Includes general principles upon which specific decisions can be based.	Some individual decisions can be made upon the basis of general principles, examples, and specific commands revealed in God's Word.

THE PATTERN OF GOD'S WILL

The first chapter of this course focused on Romans 12:1-2:

> **I beseech you therefore, brethren, by the mercies of God, that ye present
> your bodies a living sacrifice, holy, acceptable unto God which is your
> reasonable service.**
>
> **And be not conformed to this world: but be ye transformed by the renewing
> of your mind, that ye may prove what is that good, and acceptable, and
> perfect will of God. (Romans 12:1-2)**

We asked the question, "What is meant by the good, acceptable, and perfect will of God?" We
will now deal with that question, and in doing so discover the pattern of God's will.

THE PERFECT WILL OF GOD:

The perfect will of God is accomplished when a believer is in harmony with the moral,
sovereign, and individual wills of God for his life.

The believer has accepted the sovereign plan of God for his salvation through the new birth
experience. He is in harmony with the moral commandments of God's written Word. He also
has determined God's specific guidance for his individual life plan.

THE GOOD WILL OF GOD:

In the good will of God, the believer is not in the perfect plan for his life but he is within God's
sovereign will and moral will. He is not disobedient to God's revealed will, and he is still
seeking to find that perfect individual plan of God for His life.

THE ACCEPTABLE WILL OF GOD:

This believer is missing the perfect will of God for his life but is still in an acceptable area. He is
living in the permissive will of God. He may not even be concerned about God's perfect will for
His life. God is permitting him to live in this area, although it is not God's perfect will for him.

OUTSIDE THE WILL OF GOD:

The believer in this realm is in direct disobedience to God's revealed will.

AN EXAMPLE FROM SCRIPTURE

The story of Balaam in Numbers chapter 22 illustrates these realms of God's will. Read the story
before you continue with this lesson. Some men from Moab asked a prophet of God named

Balaam to go with them and prophesy against God's people, Israel. God spoke to Balaam and told him not to go:

> **And God said unto Balaam, Thou shalt not go with them; thou shalt not curse the people: for they are blessed. (Numbers 22:12)**

It was the perfect will of God for Balaam NOT to go with the men of Moab. But Balaam disobeyed God's voice and went with the men. When he did, he was functioning in disobedience outside the revealed will of God.

God desired so much for Balaam to know His will that He used a donkey to speak to him and convict him of his sin. After this God permitted Balaam to continue on with the men of Moab with orders that he was to bless rather than curse the Israelites. Balaam was now functioning in the permissive will of God.

The journey resulted in a series of trying encounters with a man named Balak. These could have been avoided if Balaam had obeyed the voice of God and never gone in the first place.

Now compare this story to the diagram of the "Pattern Of God's Will." The perfect will of God was that Balaam not go with the men of Moab. Balaam disobeyed and moved outside of the will of God. He was not in the good will of God where the believer is missing the perfect will but seeking it. He was in complete disobedience to the voice of God. The acceptable or permissive will of God permitted Balaam to continue on the journey even though it was not God's perfect will for him.

WALKING IN THE WILL

Following the born-again experience and motivated by love for God, the goal of the believer is to walk in harmony with the will of God. Often, the pattern of the believer's conformity to God's will is thought of in terms of the following diagram:

```
┌────────────────────────────────────────────────────────────────────┐
│                      Walking In The Will                            │
│                        Diagram One                                  │
│                                                                     │
│              ↗                                                      │
│           ↗     ↘                                                  │
│        ↗              ↘ New Birth Experience  → → → →              │
│     ↗                                                              │
│   ─────────────────────────────────────────────────────           │
│                                                                     │
└────────────────────────────────────────────────────────────────────┘
```

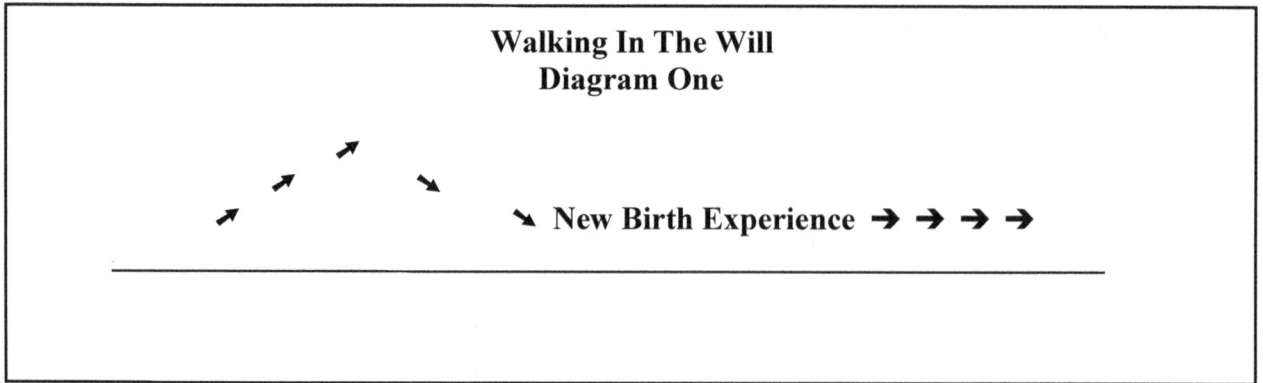

God's will is represented in this diagram by a straight unbroken line (_____).
The walk of man in relation to that will is represented by arrows.

Before the born-again experience man walks in His own way which is exactly opposite of the will of God. After the new birth experience, a believer often anticipates walking in complete harmony with God's will. Since he is a new creature in Christ, he expects to be able to conform exactly to God's will. But in the reality of daily life, his pattern of conformity looks more like this:

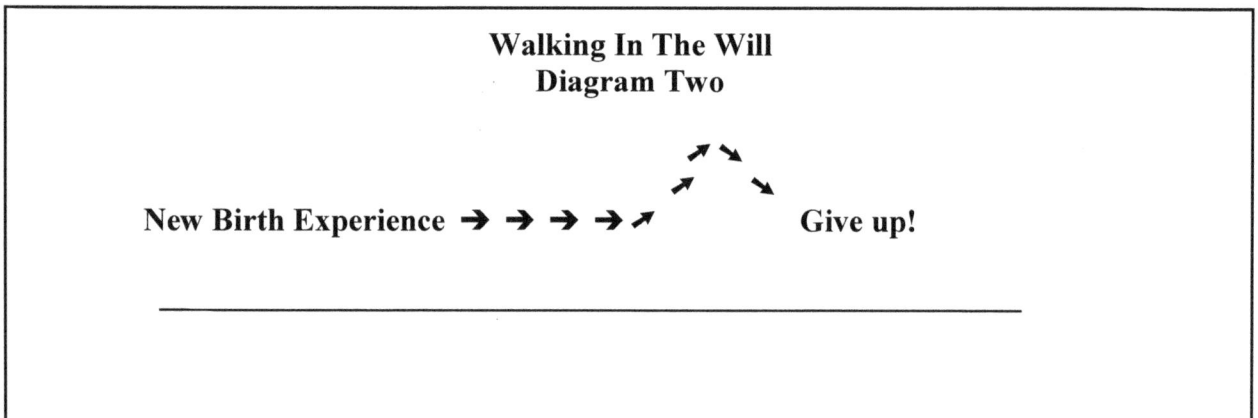

```
┌────────────────────────────────────────────────────────────────────┐
│                      Walking In The Will                            │
│                        Diagram Two                                  │
│                                                                     │
│                                        ↗ ↘                         │
│                                    ↗        ↘                      │
│   New Birth Experience  → → → → ↗              Give up!            │
│                                                                     │
│   ─────────────────────────────────────────────────               │
│                                                                     │
└────────────────────────────────────────────────────────────────────┘
```

Instead of exact conformity to God's will, the believer has an "up and down" experience. Sometimes he hears God's voice and does His will. Other times he does not. He becomes greatly discouraged when he makes mistakes and misses God's will. Some even give up in their quest to hear God's voice.

But look at this diagram again. We missed something important! While it is true that sometimes the believer misses God's will, note that the overall direction of the dotted line representing his life walk is upward. Although he may fall short of the will of God at times, the overall pattern is one of progress.

The dotted line shows how he strays from the will of God, realizes it, learns from the experience, and comes back into conformity to God's plan. Through failure as well as success, the believer is learning to hear God's voice. Through both positive and negative experiences he is continuing his growth in understanding the principles of a God-directed life.

When the will of God is perceived in this manner, it becomes a liberating relationship with Him in which you are privileged to live. The will of God ceases to become just restrictions or commandments. It becomes a challenge of learning to align your life with His plan.

A BIBLICAL EXAMPLE

Consider the example of King David. During his early life a diagram of his conformity to the will of God might have looked something like this:

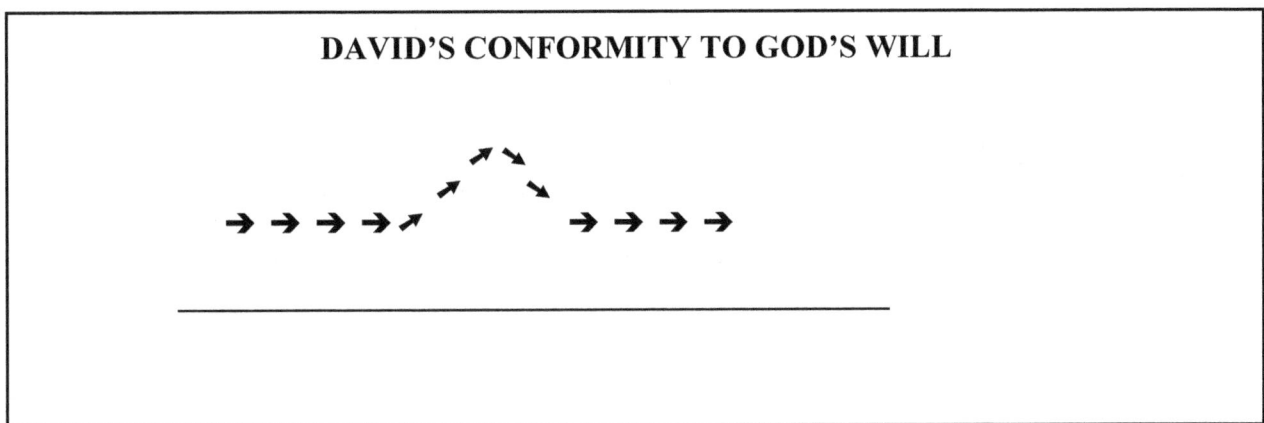

DAVID'S CONFORMITY TO GOD'S WILL

When David first became king, he walked in conformity to the will of God. God even called David a man after His own heart. But then David sinned with another man's wife who gave birth to an illegitimate child. This was in direct disobedience to God's written Word. David came before the Lord in repentance, was forgiven, and came back in line with God's will.

As we examine the ways God speaks to men in the next two chapters keep Diagram Two in mind. It is the overall pattern of your conformity to God's will that is important.

Through every experience of learning to know God's voice, both positive and negative, you can continue to advance in your ability to discern God's perfect will. Continue to strive for conformity despite occasional failures. Don't ever give up!

SELF-TEST

1.   Write the Key Verses from memory.

   _____

   _____

   _____

2.   Complete the following sentence by filling in the missing words in the blanks provided:

The two divisions of God's will discussed in this chapter were that which is revealed in

_____ _____ and that which is not revealed in_____ _____.

3.   Give a Biblical principle that would apply to the following life situation:

   "I am engaged to an unsaved man. He is kind, courteous, and has high moral
   standards. Although I am a believer and he is not, he said it would be all right for
   me to attend church after we are married and that he might even go with me. I am
   praying for God's will to be done in regards to our proposed marriage."

The Biblical principle that applies is. . .

   _____

   _____

   _____

4. List six facts about God's will which were discussed in this chapter:

   _____

   _____

   _____

   _____

   _____

5.   Is this statement true or false: If God has revealed His will regarding a certain matter in His Word you should still seek Him for confirmation. The statement is _____.

6.   Which of the following diagrams is the more realistic in showing the believer's actual conformity to the will of God:

Diagram A

New Birth Experience

Diagram B

New Birth Experience

7.   What are the four areas presented as the pattern of God's will in this chapter?

_____   _____

_____   _____

(Answers to tests are provided at the conclusion of the final chapter in this manual.)

FOR FURTHER STUDY

There are general principles and examples in God's written Word through which He communicates His will to man. There are also specific instructions in God's written Word which reveal His will in many matters. These include all the promises and commandments of the Bible. In some verses, God is so specific He actually states "This is my will for you. . . " These references are listed for you to study. You can add to this list from your own study of God's Word.

What are some of the things God has revealed as His will for you? Study the following references:

HIS PLAN FOR YOU:

And this is the will of Him that sent me, that every one which seeth the Son, and believeth on Him, may have everlasting life; and I will raise him up at the last day. (John 6:40)

And this is the Father's will which hath sent me, that of all which He hath given me I should lose nothing, but should raise it up again at the last day. (John 6:39)

All that the Father giveth me shall come to me; and Him that cometh to me I will in no wise cast out. (John 6:37)

Who gave Himself for our sins, that He might deliver us from this present evil world, according to the will of God and our Father. (Galatians 1:4)

Having predestinated us unto the adoption of children by Jesus Christ to Himself, according to the good pleasure of His will. . .

Having made known unto us the mystery of His will, according to His good pleasure which He hath purposed in Himself:

That in the dispensation of the fullness of times, He might gather together in one all things in Christ, both which are in Heaven, and which are on earth; even in Him;

In whom also we have obtained an inheritance, being predestinated according to the purpose of Him who worketh all things after the counsel of His own will. (Ephesians 1, 5, 9-11)

Of His own will begat He us with the word of truth, that we should be a kind of firstfruits of His creatures. (James 1:18)

HIS WILL FOR YOUR LOVED ONES:

The Lord is not slack concerning His promise, as some men count slackness; but is longsuffering to usward, not willing that any should perish, but that all should come to repentance. (II Peter 3:9)

HIS WILL CONCERNING YOUR SANCTIFICATION:

For this is the will of God, even your sanctification, that ye should abstain from fornication. (I Thessalonians 4:3)

HIS WILL REGARDING PRAYER AND THANKSGIVING:

Pray without ceasing. In everything give thanks for this is the will of God in Christ Jesus concerning you. (I Thessalonians 5:17-18)

And I will give unto thee the keys of the Kingdom of Heaven; and whatsoever thou shalt bind on earth shall be bound in heaven: and whatsoever thou shalt loose on earth shall be loosed in Heaven. (Matthew 16:19)

HIS WILL REGARDING YOUR LIFESTYLE:

For so is the will of God, that with well doing ye may put to silence the ignorance of foolish men. (I Peter 2:15)

HIS WILL FOR YOU REGARDING THE HOLY SPIRIT:

And it shall come to pass in the last days, saith God, I will pour out of my Spirit upon all flesh and your sons and your daughters shall prophesy, and your young men shall see visions, and your old men shall dream dreams:

An on my servants and on my handmaidens I will pour out in those days of my Spirit: and they shall prophesy. (Acts 2:17-18)

HIS WILL REGARDING YOUR CHRISTIAN WITNESS:

And Jesus said unto them, Come ye after me, and I will make you fishers of men. (Mark 1:17)
But ye shall receive power after that the Holy Ghost is come upon you: and ye shall be witnesses unto me both in Jerusalem, and in all Judaea, and in Samaria, and unto the uttermost part of the earth. (Acts 1:8)

HIS WILL REGARDING CHILDREN AND BABES IN CHRIST:

Even so, it is not the will of your Father which is in Heaven, that one of these little ones should perish. (Matthew 18:14)

HIS WILL REGARDING SUFFERING:

Let them that suffer according to the will of God commit the keeping of their souls to Him in well doing as unto a faithful creator. (I Peter 4:19)

HIS WILL REGARDING MATERIAL POSSESSIONS:

But seek ye first the Kingdom of God and His righteousness, and all these things shall be added unto you.   (Matthew 6:33)

Give and it shall be given unto you. . . (Luke 6:38)

HIS WILL REGARDING YOUR ETERNAL DESTINY:

Father I will that they also, whom thou hast given me, be with me where I am; that they may behold my glory, which thou hast given me: for thou lovedst me before the foundation the world. (John 17:24)

CHAPTER SIX

HOW GOD SPEAKS TO MAN

OBJECTIVES:

Upon completion of this chapter you will be able to:

- Write the Key Verse from memory.
- List various ways God speaks to man.
- Recognize God is not limited in His ability to communicate to man.

KEY VERSE:

> **Be ye not unwise, but understanding what the will of the Lord is.
> (Ephesians 5:17)**

INTRODUCTION

As we mentioned in the introduction of this course, the Bible is a history of methods by which God communicated to man and the response of mankind to the voice of God. This chapter examines the Biblical record to discover the methods by which God communicates to man.

THE WRITTEN WORD

As we learned in previous lessons, God speaks to man through His written Word. God does not need to speak to you concerning things already revealed in the Scriptures. When God uses other methods to communicate, they will never conflict with His written Word.

PRAYER

There are many Biblical examples of God speaking as a result of prayer. Prayer and fasting (doing without food for spiritual reasons) resulted in God speaking to Paul and Barnabas:

> **And as they ministered to the Lord and fasted, the Holy Ghost said, Separate unto me Barnabas and Saul for the work whereunto I have called them. And when they had fasted and prayed, and laid their hands on them, they sent them away. (Acts 13:2-3)**

Prayer is to include the request for the fulfillment of God's will on earth. Jesus taught His followers to pray:

Thy Kingdom come, Thy will be done in earth, as it is in Heaven. (Matthew 6:10)

Jesus prayed for direction from God prior to the selection of His disciples:

And it came to pass in those days that He went out into a mountain to pray and continued all night in prayer to God. And when it was day, He called unto Him His disciples; and of them He chose twelve, whom also He named apostles. (Luke 6:12-13)

Jesus prayed for God's will prior to His death:

. . . Saying, Father, if thou be willing, remove this cup from me: nevertheless, not my will, but thine be done. (Luke 22:42)

COUNSELORS

God communicates His will through Christian counselors. There are many Biblical examples of people seeking guidance from men of God.

The Bible states:

Where no counsel is, the people fall; but in the multitude of counselors there is safety. (Proverbs 11:14)

The way of a fool is right in his own eyes: but he that hearkeneth unto counsel is wise. (Proverbs 12:15)

CIRCUMSTANCES

God communicates His plan through circumstances. One excellent Old Testament example of this is the life of Joseph recorded in Genesis 37-50.

Joseph's brothers sold him into slavery in Egypt but he viewed this as the direction of God:

Now therefore be not grieved, nor angry with yourselves that ye sold me hither; for God did send me before you to preserve life. . . And God sent me before you to preserve you a posterity in the earth and to save your lives by a great deliverance. So now it was not you that sent me hither, but God. (Genesis 45:5-8)

Through circumstances over which Joseph had no personal control, he was used of God to save the lives of thousands of people in a time of severe famine.

Paul wrote some interesting words in I Thessalonians 2:18. He told believers at Thessalonica he was prevented from visiting them because Satan hindered. Since he could not go to them, he wrote to the church at Thessalonica. Satan's hindering resulted in the book of I Thessalonians and the important message Paul shared had greater impact than would have resulted from a visit. It has been passed down through the centuries for the benefit of all believers.

Nothing occurs apart from God's knowledge. Even when circumstances block what you might perceive to be God's will, God is still in control. God can take any deed, whether of Satan or man, and use it for His own purposes. We have a wonderful promise from God regarding circumstances:

> **And we know that all things work together for good to them that love God, to them who are the called according to His purpose. (Romans 8:28)**

(One word of warning: Caution must be used in considering circumstances alone to determine God's will. For example, God told a prophet named Jonah to go to Ninevah to preach. When he came to the waterfront, there was a boat leaving for Tarsus. He took this boat instead of going to Ninevah. He might have said, "There is a cabin open on this boat going the opposite direction, so it must be God's will that I go.")

Circumstances of life must be viewed in relation to what God reveals through other methods. God had already communicated His will to Jonah. Jonah manipulated circumstances to fulfill his own wishes.

OPEN AND CLOSED DOORS

Circumstances of life result in what has come to be called "open and closed doors." Paul wrote to the Corinthians:

> **But I will tarry at Ephesus until Pentecost. For a great door and effectual is opened unto me, and there are many adversaries. (I Corinthians 16:8-9)**

Paul decided to stay at Ephesus because through circumstances arranged by God, there was a great opportunity for Christian service open to him. He called this an open door.
On another occasion Paul records his desire to minister in certain areas, but the doors there were closed:

> **Now when they had gone throughout Phrgia and the region of Galatia and were forbidden of the Holy Ghost to preach the word in Asia,**
>
> **After they were come to Mysia, they assayed to go into Bithynia: but the Spirit suffered them not. (Acts 16:6-7)**

A closed door does not mean you have missed God's will. It does not mean it is not His will to do something. Paul later evangelized Asia. God is directing you by closing a door. He leads through closed as well as open doors. Sometimes a door is closed because it is not the right timing in the plan of God. Later, that same door may open to you.

ANGELS

Lot was given direction by angels who appeared at his home in Sodom. He was told to leave Sodom because the judgment of God was going to fall on the city (Genesis 19). An angel spoke to Philip and told him to go to Samaria (Acts 8:26). The births of John the Baptist and Jesus were announced by angels (Luke l).

There are numerous Biblical records of angels appearing to communicate the will of God to man. You can find other examples in your own study of Scriptures.

MIRACLES

A miracle is a supernatural event which is beyond the power of man to perform.

God spoke through a miracle in the event recorded in I Kings chapter 18. The prophet Elijah was told to prepare an altar before the Lord. Elijah prepared the altar and cried:

> **. . . Lord God of Abraham, Isaac, and of Israel, let it be known this day that thou art God in Israel, and that I am thy servant, and that I have done all these things at thy word. . .**

> **Then the fire of the Lord fell and consumed the burnt sacrifice, and the wood, and the stones, and the dust, and licked up the water that was in the trench.**

> **And when all the people saw it, they fell on their faces: and they said, The Lord, He is God; the Lord He is God. (I Kings 18:36,38,39)**

God used this miracle to speak to men who worshiped idols and reveal Himself as the true and living God.

God has also revealed His will through miracles in nature. A pillar of fire and a cloud in the sky gave direction to the nation of Israel by night and day as they traveled through the desert:

> **And the Lord went before them by day in a pillar of a cloud to lead them in the way; and by night in a pillar of fire, to give them light; to go by day and night.**

> **He took not away the pillar of the cloud by day, nor the pillar of fire by night, from before the people. (Exodus 13:21-22)**

You can find many other Biblical examples of God communicating to men through miracles. Watch for these in your own personal Bible study.

DREAMS

God desires so much to communicate with us that He even speaks while we sleep! God speaks in dreams. These are not the normal dreams experienced by everyone. They are supernatural dreams given by God. They are detailed, specific, and reveal His will.

The following are a few of many Biblical examples:

-God warned Abimelech in a dream about his sin of taking Abraham's wife, Sarah. Genesis 20:3

-An angel spoke to Jacob in a dream to remind him of his vow to God. Genesis 31:11-13

-God used dreams to reveal His will to Joseph. Genesis 37.

-God appeared to Solomon in a dream and gave him the opportunity to ask for whatever he desired. I Kings 3:5

-A dream was used to direct wise men to return to their country by a different route because of an evil king. Matthew 2:12-13

These are just a few of the many examples of how God communicates through dreams. You can find other examples as you continue to study this method of guidance in God's Word.

VISIONS

A vision is similar to a dream but differs because you are awake. It is like having a dream without being asleep. Visions may be seen with spiritual eyes as well as the physical eyes. This means you might not actually see it with your natural eye, but God gives you a picture of something in your spirit.

The following are a few of many Biblical examples where visions were used by God to communicate with man:

-God appeared to Abraham in a vision and made him a great promise. Genesis 15

-The book of Daniel is filled with visions (as well as dreams). God used these to reveal many things about the future of the world. He spoke to many other Old Testament prophets through visions.

-God gave Peter a vision concerning the need to take the Gospel to the Gentile nations. Acts 10

-God called Paul to Macedonia through a vision. Acts 16:9

-God spoke to Paul in the night through a vision. Acts 18:9-10

-The final book in the Bible, Revelation, is based on a vision seen by the Apostle John.

AN AUDIBLE VOICE

God spoke to Paul in an audible voice during a journey along the Damascus road. You can read the story in Acts chapter 9:

> **And he fell to the earth and head a voice saying unto him, Saul, Saul, why persecutest thou me?**
>
> **And he said, Who art thou Lord? And the Lord said, I am Jesus whom thou persecutest; it is hard for thee to kick against the pricks. (Acts 9:4-5)**

God also spoke to Samuel in an audible voice:

> **And the Lord came, and stood and called as at other times, Samuel, Samuel. The Samuel answered, Speak: for thy servant heareth. (I Samuel 3:10)**

The Bible is full of the declaration "and God said" or references to the fact that God "spoke" or "commanded." Often this was an audible voice. But there is another voice through which

God speaks. . .

THE INNER VOICE OF THE HOLY SPIRIT

More often than an audible voice, God uses the inner voice of the Holy Spirit to speak to man. This is called being "led by the Spirit":

> **For as many as are led by the Spirit of God, they are the sons of God. (Romans 8:14)**

To be "led by the Spirit" assumes a spiritual life in those being led. A soul dead in sin, with no spiritual life, cannot be led by the Holy Spirit. Being led of the Spirit also assumes an inability to lead yourself. You have learned in previous chapters that this is true.

When you experience the new birth of salvation, God gives you a new spirit which is receptive to His communications:

A new heart also will I give you, and a new spirit will I put within you: and I will take away the stony heart out of your flesh, and I will give you an heart of flesh. And I will put my spirit within you. . . (Ezekiel 36:26-27)

When you are led by the Spirit, the will of God is revealed to your spirit by the Holy Spirit. One of the ministries of the Holy Spirit is guidance:

Howbeit when He, the Spirit of truth, is come, He will guide you into all truth: for He shall not speak of Himself, but whatsoever He shall hear, that shall He speak: and He will shew you things to come. (John 16:13)

The spirit of man is that "hidden man of the heart" mentioned by Peter (I Peter 3:4). When God speaks to the inner man He is speaking to your spirit. The writer of Proverbs said the spirit of man is the candle, or lamp, of the Lord:

The spirit of man is the candle of the Lord. . . (Proverbs 20:27)

In the natural world, a candle enables you to see in darkness. In the spiritual world, God uses the candle of your spirit to direct your steps to His will. He enlightens and guides through your spirit.

Once during a journey by ship the Apostle Paul warned the captain of the vessel:

Sir, I perceive that this voyage will be with hurt and much damage, not only of the lading and ship, but also of our lives. (Acts 27:10)

Paul did not say "I had a vision." He did not claim to have a dream or that God had audibly spoken to him. His spirit had a witness from God and that witness proved to be correct.

You must train your spirit to be sensitive to God. Much time is spent on intellectual development through education. Much time is spent on physical development through exercise and athletics. But often, little time is spent on spiritual development. Your spirit can be educated just as your mind. Your spirit can develop in spiritual strength just as your body can be built and trained. You train your spirit by meditating on the Word of God:

This book of the law shall not depart out of thy mouth; but thou shalt meditate therein day and night, that thou mayest observe to do according to all that is written therein: for then thou shalt make thy way prosperous, and then thou shalt have good success. (Joshua 1:8)

God also uses the inward voice of the Holy Spirit to convict your conscience. The conscience is an inward awareness of right and wrong given by God.

Feeling is the voice of the body. God does not use how you feel to direct you. The flesh is an enemy of the spirit, so feelings can deceive you.

Reason is the voice of the mind. God's ways are often beyond human reason. His thought processes are much higher than yours.

Conscience is the voice of the spirit of man, convicting and directing you to the perfect will of God. The Holy Spirit speaks to your spirit. The spirit convicts the conscience. Through this you are brought into conformity to the will of God. When the Holy Spirit speaks to your spirit, the conscience is convicted, but if you continue to ignore it, your conscience can become "seared." This means it becomes hardened to the conviction of the Holy Spirit:

> **. . . having their conscience seared with a hot iron. . . (I Timothy 4:2)**

The book of Proverbs contains many verses that indicate God controls inner thoughts and the conscience of man to guide him into His will:

> **The preparations of the heart in man, and the answer of the tongue, is from the Lord. (Proverbs 16:1)**
>
> **A man's heart deviseth his way: but the Lord directeth his steps. (Proverbs 16:9)**
>
> **The king's heart is in the hand of the Lord as the rivers of water: He turneth it whithersoever He will. (Proverbs 21:1)**

GIFTS OF THE HOLY SPIRIT

Spiritual gifts are also used by God to speak to man. Spiritual gifts are special abilities given by the Holy Spirit. Several of these gifts enable you to receive communication from God.

There is a gift of tongues through which God speaks to man in a language he does not know. Interpretation from God follows to translate the message. The prayer language of the Holy Spirit (other tongues) is also used by the Spirit to guide you to the will of God. When you do not know how to pray regarding God's will, pray in other tongues and. . .

> **. . . He that searcheth the hearts knoweth what is in the mind of the Spirit, because He maketh intercession for the saints according to the will of God. (Romans 8:27)**

There is also the gift of prophecy which brings an immediate message from God to His people. There is a gift called discernment through which God communicates regarding the spirits operating in others. God also communicates through the gifts of wisdom and knowledge. These gifts provide divine insight about people and circumstances beyond what is known by the natural mind.

MISCELLANEOUS METHODS

Two other methods of Biblical guidance are casting of lots and the use of fleeces. We discussed both of these in previous chapters. As we learned, the casting of lots was a method of chance. It was used only prior to the giving of the Holy Spirit in a new dimension. Its use is never again recorded after the guiding ministry of the Holy Spirit became available (Acts 2). We learned that a fleece is only mentioned once in the Bible. It was used by Gideon at a time of great national crisis. It was a miraculous sign used for confirmation, not direction.

GOD IS NOT LIMITED

God does not always speak in the same way. We try to limit God to a set pattern. Because God has spoken in a certain way one time, we believe He will always direct in the same way. But as we have learned in this chapter, God has many methods of communicating with man. God is not limited by a set pattern. Consider these examples:

MOSES:

When Moses was leading the nation of Israel across the dessert to the land God promised them, providing water for two million people was a major challenge. On one occasion God told Moses to strike a rock with his rod. When he did, water poured out of the rock. On another occasion when the Israelites were thirsty God wanted Moses to speak to the rock. Instead, Moses struck the rock as he had done previously. This was displeasing to God, and Moses was punished. This story illustrates the importance of waiting for guidance from God even when facing a familiar situation. God is not limited to any previous pattern which you have experienced.

(Note: You might think God was unjust to punish Moses for such a little thing as striking the rock instead of speaking to it. The rock held symbolic meaning. It represented the Lord Jesus Christ and the living water of redemption which would burst forth through His death. Jesus was stricken once and for all. There was no need for another striking. It was the importance of this symbolism that made the offense of Moses so great.)

ELIJAH:

God used many supernatural methods to communicate to the Prophet Elijah. Once Elijah had a unique experience which illustrated the importance of knowing God's voice. Elijah was told to go and stand on a certain mountain and wait for God to speak to him. This is what happened:

And behold, the Lord passed by, and a great and strong wind rent the mountains, and brake in pieces the rocks before the Lord; but the Lord was not in the wind: and after the wind an earthquake; but the Lord was not in the earthquake:

And after the earthquake a fire: but the Lord was not in the fire: and after the fire a still small voice. (I Kings 19:11-12)

There were several supernatural events in this account. There was a wind, an earthquake, and fire. These were methods by which God had previously communicated with Elijah. But this time, God did not speak in all the glorious events that occurred. He spoke in a still small voice. This could have been either an audible voice or a silent voice in Elijah's spirit.

PAUL:

God used many ways to direct the Apostle Paul during his missionary ministry:

-On the Damascus road Paul was directed by a bright light and a voice from Heaven. Acts 9:1-8
-When a plot was formed to murder Paul, he was warned by believers who were used of God to help him escape. Acts 9:20-25
-Barnabas was used by God to establish relationships between Paul and the other disciples. Acts 9:20-28
-Believers were used of God to help Paul escape the angry Grecians. Acts 9:29-30
-When Paul met an occultist, God gave him discernment to bring deliverance. Acts 13:6-12
-Prayer and the Holy Spirit guided Paul into a special missionary ministry. Acts 13:2-4
-Personal prophecy by Agabus confirmed the experience that awaited Paul in Jerusalem. Acts 21:10-14
-God spoke to Paul through dreams and visions. Acts 22:18; 26:19; 27:23-24
-An effectual door of service for the Lord caused Paul to change his personal plans. I Corinthians 16:8-10

PHILIP:

And the angel of the Lord spake unto Philip, saying, Arise and go toward the south unto the way that goeth down from Jerusalem unto Gaza, which is desert.

And he arose and went; and behold, a man of Ethiopia, an unich of great authority under Candace, queen of the Ethiopians, who had the charge of all her treasure, and had come to Jerusalem for to worship, was returning and

sitting in his chariot reading Essaias the prophet. Then the spirit said unto Philip, Go near, and join thyself to this chariot. (Acts 8:26-29)

God spoke to Philip the first time through an angel. The second time He spoke through the Holy Spirit and Philip responded immediately. He did not wait for confirmation from an angel the second time God spoke just because that method had been used previously.

DAVID:

When David was a young man, he battled an enemy of God's people named Goliath. Although Goliath was a giant and well armed, God told David not to use traditional weapons of warfare. Instead, David used a sling shot. In a glorious victory, David brought down the enemy with one well-directed shot which struck him in the forehead. In later years David could have been slain by a giant named Isbibenob if his nephew Abishai had not come to his aid. Are we to conclude that God was with David when he met Goliath, but not when he confronted the second giant? No. God simply used a different method. The first time God used David's skill with a sling. The second time He used Abishai's military skill.

When God does not choose to speak to you as He has in the past, do not become frustrated. If His will for you in a similar situation is not identical to what it was previously, do not become confused. God is not restricted to certain communication patterns. The great Creator is also a great Communicator. His methods are unlimited.

SELF-TEST

1. Write the Key Verse from memory.

_____

_____

2. Give one of the several Scriptural examples discussed in this lesson which confirm God is not limited and does not always speak in the same way.

_____

3. List the twelve ways discussed in this chapter as Biblical methods God uses to speak to man.

_____ _____ _____ _____ _____ _____

_____ _____ _____ _____ _____ _____

4. Read the following statements. If the statement is True, write the letter T on the blank provided in front of it. If a statement is False, write the letter F on the blank provided in front of it.

a._____If you encounter a "closed door" it means you must have missed God's will.

b._____Jesus did not pray for God's will because He already knew it.

c._____Joseph felt he was a victim of circumstances and resented it.

d._____Circumstances are the best indication of the will of God.

e._____Jonah manipulated circumstances to fulfill his own will instead of God's will.

f._____God's other methods of communication will always agree with His written Word.

(Answers to tests are provided at the conclusion of the final chapter in this manual.)

FOR FURTHER STUDY

1. Study the following prayers for guidance:

    Psalms 25:4
    Colossians 1:9
    Psalms 86:11
    Colossians 4:12
    Ephesians 6:18-20

2. God communicates His will to man, but sometimes man is too hasty in making decisions. Study the following examples of men who acted too hastily, not allowing God opportunity to communicate His will to them:

    Moses slaying the Egyptian: Exodus 2

    Joshua's league with the Gibeonites: Joshua 9

    Abraham and Ishmael: Abraham did not wait for the promised heir: Genesis 16

3. Read the book of Acts. Make a list of the different ways God communicated with men in the early church.

    _____

    _____

    _____

    _____

    _____

    _____

    _____

    _____

    _____

CHAPTER SEVEN

THE BUSH STILL BURNS

OBJECTIVES:

Upon completion of this chapter you will be able to:

- Write the Key Verse from memory.
- List steps for finding God's will.
- Explain how to have assurance of the will of God.
- Identify three keys for receiving direction from God.

KEY VERSE:

> **Trust in the Lord with all thine heart; and lean not to thine own understanding. In all thy ways acknowledge Him and He shall direct thy paths. (Proverbs 3:5-6)**

INTRODUCTION

In the previous chapter we examined the Biblical record of God's communication with man in the past. But the question is, does God still speak to men today?

The Apostle Paul summarized:

> **God, who at sundry times and in divers manners spake in time past unto the fathers by the prophets.**
>
> **Hath in these last days spoken unto us by His Son, who He hath appointed heir of all things, by whom also He made the worlds. (Hebrews 1:1-2)**

God spoke in various ways in times past. He continued to speak to men in the time of Paul. Paul said the greatest message God ever communicated was through His Son, Jesus Christ.

TIMES PAST: THE BURNING BUSH

God communicated His message in Biblical times by many methods. One method He used is recorded in Exodus chapter 3:

> **Now Moses kept the flock of Jethro his father in law the priest of Midian: and he led the flock to the backside of the desert, and came to the mountain of God, even to Horeb.**

And the angel of the Lord appeared unto him in a flame of fire out of the midst of a bush: and he looked, and behold, the bush burned with fire and the bush was not consumed.

And Moses said, I will now turn aside, and see this great sight, why the bush is not burnt.

And when the Lord saw that he turned aside to see, God called unto him out of the midst of the bush and said, Moses, Moses. (Exodus 3:1-4)

From a burning bush which was not consumed, God to Moses called Moses to deliver the nation of Israel from Egyptian bondage. Yes, God definitely spoke to men in times past!

THE PRESENT TIME: THE BUSH STILL BURNS

But does God still speak to men today in such miraculous ways? Were these forms of communication limited to Old Testament times before the infilling of the Holy Spirit was given?

The bush still burns! You may not actually experience this specific form of guidance given Moses, but God still speaks to men in miraculous ways just as He did in Old Testament times.

In Hebrews 1:1-2 Paul pointed out that God continues to speak to the world through Jesus Christ. Not only does God speak through the written Word which records the life and teachings of Jesus, but Jesus promised:

Howbeit, when He, the Spirit of truth is come, He will guide you into all truth: for He shall not speak of Himself, but whatsoever He shall hear, that shall He speak: and He will shew you things to come. (John 16:13)

The Holy Spirit continues to speak by Jesus communicating God's message to man.

After the coming of the Holy Spirit in Acts 2, special revelations from God continued just as in Old Testament times. People dreamed dreams, saw visions, talked with angels, heard the audible voice of God, and experienced other miraculous revelations from God.

Miraculous communication from God did not cease with the coming of the Holy Spirit. The Holy Spirit just added a new dimension of guidance. That dimension included inward direction, intercession according to the will God through the prayer language of other tongues, and special spiritual gifts through which God speaks.

The final book of the Bible, Revelation, is an extended record of a vision God gave to the Apostle John. Right up to the end of His written Word, God is speaking to man in miraculous ways.

God continues to speak to man through these methods. Modern church history contains many well documented instances of miraculous communications from God to man because. . .

Jesus Christ the same yesterday, and to day, and for ever. (Hebrews 13:8)

WHAT IF THERE IS NO BUSH?

But what happens if God does not choose to speak to you through a miraculous method. What if you do not experience a dream, vision or miracle? What if He does not speak to you through an audible voice or through supernatural gifts of prophecy, tongues, or interpretation? What if there is no burning bush?

Some people wait all their lives for a supernatural revelation from God. Multitudes of believers waste their lives, immobile and ineffective, waiting for some unusual or dramatic message from God.

The early church did not do this. They rejoiced when God chose to lead through miraculous methods, but in the many decisions of everyday life they were not guided by angels, dreams, and visions. Yet they moved ahead as a mighty force for God.

So, what do you do if there is no burning bush? Here are seven steps to finding God's will:

1.   PRAY:

Pray for God's direction in your life. Jesus taught His followers that part of the regular pattern of prayer was to be for the will of God to be done:

> **Thy Kingdom come, Thy will be done in earth, as it is in Heaven.**
> **(Matthew 6:10)**

When you pray, express your desire for God to reveal His will to you. Moses did this:

> **Now therefore, I pray thee, if I have found grace in thy sight, shew me now**
> **thy way, that I may know thee, that I may find grace in thy sight: and**
> **consider that this nation is thy people. (Exodus 33:13)**

David did this:

> **Shew me thy ways, O Lord; teach me thy paths. (Psalms 25:4)**

Ask for wisdom to make the right choices:

> **If any of you lack wisdom (in determining the will of God) let him ask of**

God, that giveth to all men liberally and upbraideth not; and it shall be given him.

But let him ask in faith, nothing wavering. For he that wavereth is like a wave of the sea driven with the wind and tossed.

For let not that man think that he shall receive anything of the Lord.
(James 1:5-7)

Request the prayers of other believers. God often reveals His will through spiritual gifts exercised in group prayer meetings. Paul and Barnabas received confirmation of their calling to missionary service in such a gathering.

2.   STUDY THE SCRIPTURES:

Earnestly search God's written Word to determine if specific guidance is given for your situation. Determine if there are general Biblical principles or biographical examples which apply.

Searching the Scriptures does not mean letting the Bible fall open and taking the first verse your eyes fall on as your answer. Searching the Scriptures is a detailed examination of the Word and application of its principles to the decisions you must make. Every open door, every opportunity, every other leading you think might be from the Lord should first be tested by the written Word of God. Jesus used this principle. When He was tempted by Satan to act apart from God's will he answered repeatedly "It is written. . ." (Matthew 4). He analyzed everything on the basis of God's written Word.

As you search the Scriptures, be sure to study the many promises for direction. We have listed some of these in the "For Further Study" section of this chapter. As you study these passages it will increase your faith that God does speak and that you can know His voice.

3.   LISTEN TO THE INNER VOICE OF THE HOLY SPIRIT:

Through prayer and study of the Scriptures, God speaks His will into your spirit by the inner voice of the Holy Spirit. We discussed this at length in the last chapter. Part of the "voice of the Holy Spirit" is the prayer language of other tongues. When you are not certain of God's will in a matter, pray in the prayer language of the Holy Spirit.

The Holy Spirit knows the perfect will of God and will pray through you in harmony with that will:

> **. . .He that searcheth the hearts knoweth what is in the mind of the spirit, because He maketh intercession for the saints according to the will of God. (Romans 8:27)**

Remember--Jesus said that the Holy Spirit would "shew you things to come." This means He reveals God's plan to you. He guides you according to the will of God.

4.   SEEK CHRISTIAN COUNSEL:

As we mentioned in the last chapter, God uses Christian counselors to assist believers in the decision making process.   The Bible states:

>**Where there is no counsel, the people fall; but in the multitude of counselors there is a safety. (Proverbs 11:14)**

>**The way of a fool is right in his own eyes: but he that hearkeneth unto counsel is wise. (Proverbs 12:15)**

It is important that believers seek counsel only from mature Christians. Never seek counsel from secular psychologists or psychiatrists. They will give worldly counsel. They are "blind leaders of the blind":

>**Woe unto you, ye blind guides. . . (Matthew 23:16)**

>**Blessed is the man that walketh not in the counsel of the ungodly. . .
>(Psalms 1:1)**

Never seek counsel from new Christians, as they lack experience and spiritual maturity.

Some people only go to a counselor hoping to get them to agree with their own opinions. You will receive little benefit from counseling if this is your attitude. Some believers consult many counselors comparing the counsel they receive. They appear to be taking a poll as to how many are in favor of one course of action as opposed to another. This is not the purpose of counseling. Most important, always remember that all counsel of man must agree with the written Word of God.

5.   ANALYZE THE CIRCUMSTANCES:

Analyze the circumstances relating to the decision you need to make. These should be considered in relation to the guidance God gives through prayer, study of the Word, the inner voice of the Spirit, and Christian counsel.

Circumstances should not be used alone to determine God's will, but they do define the context of the decision which is to be made. Sometimes circumstances limit choices or provide opportunity for new direction in life.

6.   USE THE BIBLICAL KEYS TO DIRECTION:

In the natural world, keys open doors. In the spiritual world, God has provided keys to open the door to His will. The keys are found in the book of Proverbs:

Trust in the Lord with all thine heart; and lean not unto thine own understanding. In all thy ways acknowledge Him, and He shall direct thy paths. (Proverbs 3:5-6)

The First Key: Trust.

Do not fear what God may ask of you. Know that His plan for you is best. Certainly, men should be able to trust one who would give His only Son to die for them. Your trust must be in the Lord and not in man:

Thus saith the Lord, Cursed by be the man that trusteth in man and maketh flesh his arm, and whose heart departeth from the Lord. (Jeremiah 17:5)

The Second Key: Lean Not To Your Own Understanding.

Do not depend on your own human reasoning. This does not mean there is no place for intelligent judgment. The book of Proverbs is filled with commands to use understanding and common sense. God is not saying you should abandon sound judgment. He is simply saying do not depend solely on human reasoning when you are seeking the will of God.

When David was returning the ark to Jerusalem, He did not ask God for direction. He leaned on his own understanding and started to move the ark in the most practical way possible (II Samuel 6:1-7).

But this was not God's way and judgment fell. It was God's will to bring the ark back to Jerusalem, but David had not aligned God's will with His way. This is an important principle of guidance.

The Third Key: In All Thy Ways Acknowledge Him.

To acknowledge God in all ways is to honor Him in thought, word, and deed. Give Him first place in your life:

That in all things He might have the preeminence. (Colossians 1:18)

Joshua made a serious mistake when "he asked not counsel of the mouth of the Lord" concerning a treaty with the Gibeonites (Joshua 9). His decision resulted in an alliance with an ungodly nation, something which was forbidden by God.

The three keys. . .

    -Trust in the Lord with all thine heart. . .
    -Lean not to thine own understanding. . .
    -In all thy ways acknowledge Him. . ..

These keys open the door. . ..And He shall direct thy paths.

7.   CHOOSE THE WAY OF WISDOM:

In decisions specifically dealt with in the written Word of God, you must always make a decision consistent with the revealed Word. In other decisions, after prayer, study of the Word, listening to the voice of the Spirit, seeking counsel, and analyzing the circumstances, you can make a choice according to "the way of wisdom." (Remember--you prayed for wisdom from God. Now you make a choice on the basis of that wisdom.)

The way of wisdom is the option in any decision which offers the greatest opportunity for spiritual advancement in every area of life. It is the option in harmony with what God has revealed through prayer, the written Word, the inner voice of the Holy Spirit, and Christian counsel.

Ability to recognize the way of wisdom increases through spiritual maturity:

> **For when for the time ye ought to be teachers, ye have need that one teach you again which be the first principles of the oracles of God: and are become such as have need of milk and not of strong meat.**
>
> **For every one that useth milk is unskillful in the word of righteousness; for he is a babe.**
>
> **But strong meat belongeth to them that are of full age, even those who by reason of use have their senses exercised to discern both good and evil. (Hebrews 5:12-14)**

Spiritual maturity comes from relationship with God, prayer, and meditation in His written Word.

ASSURANCE OF THE WILL OF GOD

> **And let the peace (soul harmony which comes) from the Christ rule (act as umpire continually) in your hearts-deciding and settling with finality all questions that arise in your minds- (in that peaceful state) to which (as members of Christ's) one body you were also called (to live). . .
> (Colossians 3:15 The Amplified Version)**

An umpire is a person responsible for reviewing a sports event to determine if the game is being playing according to the rules.

In the spiritual world, the peace of God is the umpire of the will of God. Your actions and decisions are reviewed. When they are in harmony with God's will, you will have peace in your spirit. When you are confused or frustrated, do not act. Wait until you receive peace concerning the decision you are making. Lack of peace is a signal from the umpire that something is wrong:

For God is not the author of confusion, but of peace. . . (I Corinthians 14:33)

A STEP AT A TIME

One final important principle in the matter of God's will is to recognize God reveals His plan a step at a time. This means He does not reveal the entire plan for your life, with all the details, at one time. God does not just speak once in a lifetime to you. You cannot develop a relationship with someone on the basis of one conversation. Relationship is a continuing process of communication. God continues to speak, and you increase in your ability to recognize His voice.

God has reasons for revealing His will a step at a time. Often, you are not ready to know the whole plan because it might overwhelm you or cause feelings of inadequacy for the task ahead. Jesus once said to His disciples:

> **I have many things to say unto you, but ye cannot bear them now.**
> **(John 16:12)**

God told Israel that he would defeat their enemies in Canaan "little by little" as they were ready and able to assume responsibility for the new land He was giving them.

God also does not reveal His entire plan because we tend to worry over the future. The Bible warns:

> **Take therefore no thought for the morrow; for the morrow shall take**
> **thought for the things of itself. (Matthew 6:34)**

Do not worry about the future. Make only the decisions necessary for today. The future is controlled by God. This does not mean you should not do wise planning for the future. But you are not to worry about it. What is important is to live in the revealed will of God for this day. Learn to hear His voice in your daily Christian walk. A daily walk in His will results in a life-long walk in His will.

God does not reveal His total plan because He wants you to learn to live by faith. It is easier to take the first step if one knows where the path is headed. It is not as easy to make a step of faith into the unknown.

The Bible states regarding Abraham:

> **By faith, Abraham, when he was called to go out into a place which he should after receive for an inheritance obeyed; and he went out, not knowing whither he went. (Hebrews 11:8)**

Nothing can build faith in God better that walking a step at a time. Taking a step at a time as God reveals it means you cannot move too hastily. Moses moved too quickly and killed an Egyptian. Abraham moved ahead of God's plan and tried to substitute Ishmael for the chosen heir.

The book of Esther stresses the importance of waiting on God. The people of God were in danger of being destroyed by an evil man named Haaman. He had asked the King to destroy all Jews.

Queen Esther was aware of the plot. She knew it was not God's will for the Jewish people to be destroyed, but she did not act in haste. She waited until God gave her a plan and then she waited an extra day before talking to the King. During that waiting period an important thing happened. The King discovered that Mordeacai, a Jew, had saved his life from a plot to murder him.

When this was made known, then Esther revealed Haaman's plot against the Jews. The king acted against Haaman's plan, the Jews were saved, and Haaman was punished for his evil--all because Esther waited one more day before acting.

THE BUSH STILL BURNS

In a spiritual sense, the bush still burns. God still guides us and desires to speak to us:

> **Call unto me, and I will answer thee, and shew thee great and mighty things, which thou knowest not. (Jeremiah 33:3)**

God wants to reveal His will and communicate His plans. He continues to guide and direct. God is a still God who speaks if you will only listen.

SELF-TEST

1.   Write the Key Verse from memory.

_____

2.   What is the assurance God gives when a believer is functioning in His perfect will?

_____

3.   What are the three keys to determining God's will given in Proverbs 3:5-6?

      _____   _____   _____

4.   What does it mean to "acknowledge God" in all ways?

_____

5.   List seven steps for finding God's will discussed in this chapter.

      _____   _____   _____

      _____   _____   _____

                          _____

6.   Read the following statements. If the statement is True, write the letter T on the blank provided in front of it. If the statement is False, write the letter F on the blank in front of it.

      a._____ An excellent method of using the Bible to determine God's will is to open it at random and take the first verse that stands out to you as your answer.

      b._____ God usually reveals His entire plan for your life, with all the details, in one miraculous revelation.

      c._____ God does not speak today through dreams, visions, and other similar miraculous methods.

(Answers to tests are provided at the conclusion of the final chapter in this manual.)

FOR FURTHER STUDY

1. Compare Proverbs 3:5-6 and Romans 12:1-2. There are two positive commandments in each passage (things to do) and one negative commandment (something not to do). List these on the following chart:

    Proverbs 3:5-6   **Romans 12:1-2**

    Positive Commandment:

    Negative Commandment:

    Positive Commandment:

2. Rev. George Mueller was a great spiritual leader who founded and directed an orphanage in England and various missionary works throughout the world. In his writings, Rev. Mueller set forth his formula for determining the will of God:

    "I seek at the beginning to get my heart into such a state that it has no will of its own in regards to a given matter.

    Nine-tenths of the trouble with people is just here. Nine-tenths of the difficulties are overcome when our hearts are ready to do the Lord's will, whatever it may be. When one is truly in this state, it is usually but a little way to the knowledge of His will.

    Having done this, I do not leave the result to feeling or a single impression. If I do so, I make myself liable to great delusions.

    I seek the will of the Spirit of God through, or in connection with, the Word of God. The Spirit and the Word must be combined. If I look to the Spirit alone without the Word, I lay myself open to great delusions also. if the Holy Ghost guides us at all, He will do it according to the Scriptures and never contrary to them.

    Next, I take into account providential circumstances. These often plainly indicate God's will in connection with His Word and Spirit. I ask God in prayer to reveal His will to me aright. Thus, through prayer, the study of the Word, and reflection, I come to a deliberate judgment according to the best of my ability and knowledge, and if my mind is thus at peace and continues so after two or three more repetitions, I proceed accordingly.

    In trivial matters and in transactions involving most important issues, I have found this method always effective."

3. God has given many promises in His Word regarding guidance. Study the following references:

    Psalms 3:8; 5:8; 25:5,9:12; 27:11; 31:3; 32:8; 37:23; 48:14; 61:2; 73:24; 78:52,72; 85:8, 13; 107:7; 139:10,24; 142:3; 143:10
    Proverbs 3:6; 4:11; 8:20; 11:3,15; 16:9; 21:29; 23:19
    Ecclesiastes 10:10
    Isaiah 45:13; 58:11; 61:8
    John 10:3; 16:13
    Ephesians 5:17
    Colossians 1:9; 4:12

4. One of the greatest examples of guidance was God's leading the nation of Israel from Egypt to the promised land. You can read about this in the following passages:

    Exodus 13:17, 18, 21: 15:13
    Deuteronomy 8:2, 15; 29:5; 32:10;
    I Chronicles 11:2
    II Chronicles 25:11
    II Samuel 5:2
    Nehemiah 9:12
    Psalms 77:20; 78:14, 53; 80:1; 106:9; 107:7; 136:16
    Isaiah 48:21; 63:12-14
    Jeremiah 2:6, 17
    Hebrews 8:9

5. Here is a simple pattern to follow when making a decision:
    -Contradiction: Make sure there is no contradiction to God's Word in the decision you are making.
    -Control: Control your emotions. Do not make decisions in anger, despondency, fear, etc. based on your mood at the moment.
    -Counsel: Seek Godly counsel regarding the decision.
    -Circumstances: Analyze both positive and negative situations that relate to the decision. God often uses circumstances to direct your life.
    -Compulsion: Analyze your passions. Sometimes, God gives you a compelling desire to do something in order to direct you to His will. If it is from Him, it will always be in harmony with His Word.
    -Conscience: Check your inner warning system--your conscience--which is a God-given alarm that lets you know if you are heading the right direction.
    -Contentment: Be sure that you have the peace of the Holy Spirit which results when you make right decisions.

CHAPTER EIGHT

QUESTIONABLE PRACTICES

OBJECTIVES:

Upon completion of this chapter you will be able to:

- Write the Key Verse from memory.
- Explain what is meant by the term "questionable practices."
- Give Scriptural guidelines for decision making on questionable practices.
- Distinguish between a "weaker brother" and a "stronger brother."
- Give Scriptural guidelines for dealing with a "weaker brother."
- Give Scriptural guidelines for handling disagreements between believers.
- Give Scriptural guidelines for resolving offenses between believers.

KEY VERSE:

> **Whether therefore ye eat, or drink, or whatsoever ye do, do all to the glory of God. (I Corinthians 10:31)**

INTRODUCTION

This chapter concerns decision making about questionable practices. The term is defined and discussion includes guidelines for dealing with questionable practices, dealing with weaker brethren, handling disagreements between believers, and resolving offenses.

QUESTIONABLE PRACTICES

In every culture there are certain practices which are questionable. These are practices which are not specifically mentioned in Scripture as being either wrong or right for a follower of Jesus.

You can easily think of such practices in your own culture. They might include activities of leisure or entertainment. They may be clubs or organizations to which you could choose to belong. These practices include certain habits and choices of what you eat or drink. They may be questions on which days to worship or holy days.

How do you determine the will of God regarding questionable practices when specific guidance on such matters is not given in the Bible? Ask yourself these questions:

DOES IT GLORIFY GOD?

Perhaps the most important principle by which to judge a questionable practice is to ask the question, "Does it glorify God?"

The Bible indicates all you do should glorify the Lord:

> **Whether therefore ye eat, or drink, or whatsoever ye do, do all to the glory of God. (I Corinthians 10:31)**

> **And whatsoever ye do in word or deed, do all in the name of the Lord Jesus, giving thanks to God and the Father by Him. (Colossians 3:17)**

> **And whatsoever ye do, do it heartily, as to the Lord, and not unto men; Knowing that of the Lord ye shall receive the reward of the inheritance: for ye serve the Lord Christ. (Colossians 3:23-24)**

WHAT IS YOUR MOTIVATION?

Why do you want to engage in this practice? What is your reason or motive for doing it? Even a good activity can be done with a wrong motive. For example, James gives an illustration of a wrong motive for prayer:

> **Ye ask, and receive not, because ye ask amiss, that ye may consume it upon your lusts. (James 4:3)**

Praying is certainly not wrong but the motives for some requests are improper. The motivation described in this verse is the wish to fulfill lustful desires.

IS IT NECESSARY?

Paul states that while some things may be considered lawful (not in violation of God's written Word), you should consider whether they are really necessary. He states:

> **All things are lawful unto me, but all things are not expedient. . .**
> **(I Corinthians 6:12)**

WILL IT PROMOTE SPIRITUAL GROWTH?

Many activities can hinder spiritual growth. Other activities can become so time consuming that they choke out spiritual growth:

> **And these are they which are sown among thorns; such as hear the word.**

> **And the cares of this world, and the deceitfulness of riches, and the lusts of other things entering in, choke the word, and it becometh unfruitful. (Mark 4:18-19)**

> **And that which fell among thorns are they, which when they have heard, go forth, and are choked with cares and riches and pleasures of this life, and bring no fruit to perfection. (Luke 8:14)**

Ask yourself: "Will this activity hinder or promote my spiritual development?"

Activities that hinder spiritual development become weights which interfere with the spiritual race God has set before you:

> **Wherefore seeing we also are compassed about with so great a cloud of witnesses, let us lay aside every weight and the sin which doth so easily beset us, and let us run with patience the race that is set before us. (Hebrews 12:1)**

IS IT AN ENSLAVING HABIT?

When considering a questionable practice, ask yourself "Will this practice enslave me to a habit?" An enslaving habit is one which controls you. You feel you cannot get along without it and you have difficulty giving it up.

Paul comments regarding enslaving habits:

> **. . .All things are lawful unto me, but I will not be brought under the power of any. (I Corinthians 6:12)**

Any activity which is enslaving physically, mentally, spiritually, or habitually demands valuable time should be avoided.

IS IT A COMPROMISE?

Paul asks in II Corinthians 6:14, ". . . what communion hath light with darkness?"

Will the questionable practice you are considering be a spiritual compromise? Will you be engaging in activities of the world or accepting its standards by doing this thing? The Bible commands:

> **Wherefore come out from among them, and be ye separate, saith the Lord, and touch not the unclean thing; and I will receive you. (II Corinthians 6:17)**

WILL IT LEAD TO TEMPTATION?

Jesus taught us to pray "lead us not into temptation." It is useless to pray this prayer and then by means of a questionable activity deliberately place yourself in a place of temptation. The Bible warns:

>**Let no man say when he is tempted, I am tempted of God, for God cannot be tempted with evil, neither tempteth He any man;**
>
>**But every man is tempted when he is drawn away of his own lust and enticed.**
>
>**Then when lust hath conceived, it bringeth forth sin; and sin, when it is finished, bringeth forth death. (James 1:13-15)**

Temptation is different from a trial of faith. A trial of faith occurs when a believer faces a difficult situation through no fault of his own. The situation tries his faith in God. God permits trials to strengthen your faith and bring spiritual maturity.

But God does not tempt man. Temptation is the desire to do wrong. Temptation comes when you do not control your thoughts and actions properly or when Satan entices you to do evil. Some questionable practices may put you in situations of temptation. If you yield to the temptation, lust results in sin, and sin results in spiritual death.

DOES IT GIVE THE APPEARANCE OF EVIL?

Does the practice you are considering give an appearance of evil to others? The Bible commands:

>**Abstain from all appearance of evil. (I Thessalonians 5:22)**

DOES IT VIOLATE YOUR CONSCIENCE?

When making a decision regarding questionable practices, you should be fully persuaded the choice you make is right. In New Testament times believers disagreed over whether or not it was right to eat meat since meat had been used for sacrifices under the Old Testament law. These sacrifices were used as atonement for man's sin before Jesus gave His life as the final and complete sacrifice for sin. Because meat was used for sacrifices there were laws against eating certain meats. Paul wrote regarding this question:

>**And he that doubteth is damned if he eat, because he eateth not of faith: for whatsoever is not of faith is sin. (Romans 14:23)**

The principle is that you must be fully persuaded in questionable matters that what you are doing is right. If you have doubts, then it becomes sin for you to engage in such practices.

HOW WILL IT AFFECT OTHERS?

This leads to the final guideline in regards to questionable practices. How will engaging in this activity affect others? Will it edify others? To edify means to instruct, build up, or improve spiritually. The Bible states:

> **Let us therefore follow after the things which make for peace and things wherewith one may edify another. (Romans 14:19)**

Does this activity contribute in a positive way to the spiritual development of others? Paul writes:

> **All things are not lawful for me, but all things are not expedient: all things are lawful for me, but all things edify not. (I Corinthians 10:23)**

Some practices in which you might engage may cause other believers to be hindered in their spiritual walk. Again, speaking on the question of eating meat, Paul wrote:

> **Wherefore, if meat make my brother to offend, I will eat no flesh while the world standeth lest I make my brother to offend. (I Corinthians 8:13)**

Paul did not consider it wrong to eat meat. But he would not eat it if it hindered a weaker brother in the Lord. A weaker brother is a believer who, because of weakness of faith, knowledge, or conscience can be affected by the example of a stronger brother. He can be influenced to sin against his conscience and his spiritual progress can be hindered.

A stronger believer is one who, because of his understanding of freedom in certain areas and the strength of his conviction, exercises liberty with good conscience. He is not influenced by the differing opinions of others.

Any action by a stronger brother which ordinarily would be permissible is wrong if it influences a weaker brother to sin against his conscience or hinders his spiritual progress. Paul wrote:

> **It is good neither to eat flesh nor to drink wine nor any thing whereby thy brother stumbleth, or is offended, or is made weak. (Romans 14:21)**

SUMMARY: DECISION MAKING ON QUESTIONABLE PRACTICES

The following chart summarizes Biblical guidelines for decision making on questionable practices:

Ask Yourself. . .	Biblical Reference
Does it glorify God?	I Corinthians 10:31; Colossians 3:17,23
What is your motivation?	James 4:3
Is it necessary?	I Corinthians 6:12
Will it promote spiritual growth?	Mark 4:18,19; Luke 8:14; Hebrews 12:1
Is it an enslaving habit?	I Corinthians 6:12
Is it a compromise?	II Corinthians 6:17
Will it lead to temptation?	James 1:13-15
Does it give the appearance of evil?	I Thessalonians 5:22
Does it violate your conscience?	Romans 14:23
How will it affect others?	Romans 14:19,21; I Corinthians 8:13; 10:23

WHEN BELIEVERS DIFFER

Study Romans 14:1 through 15:2. These verses reveal believers will sometimes have differences in opinion. Such differences often arise over questionable practices not specifically dealt with in God's Word as being either right or wrong.

This passage explains that such differences will not result in harm if we love one another and continue to search the Scriptures. Romans 14 gives the following guidelines for dealing with disagreements between believers in matters not specifically covered in the written Word of God:

DISTINGUISH BETWEEN MATTERS OF COMMAND AND FREEDOM:

Romans 14:14 indicates that when believers differ it is important to distinguish between matters of command and freedom. Concerning matters of freedom not specifically dealt with in God's Word, Paul writes:

> **I know, and am persuaded by the Lord Jesus, that there is nothing unclean of itself: but to him that esteemeth any thing to be unclean, to him it is unclean. (Romans 14:14)**

In matters of command recorded in the written Word of God, we should all conform to the same pattern. In other matters, freedom of choice may be exercised.

CULTIVATE YOUR OWN CONVICTIONS:

You must cultivate your own convictions regarding questionable practices. In regards to observing holy days Paul wrote:

> **One man esteemeth one day above another; another esteemeth every day alike. Let every man be fully persuaded in his own mind. (Romans 14:5)**

Use the guidelines given in the previous section of this chapter to help you determine your own convictions on questionable matters.

ALLOW OTHERS FREEDOM TO DETERMINE THEIR CONVICTIONS:

Even if others differ from you, allow them freedom to determine their own convictions on questionable matters:

> **But why dost thou judge thy brother? Or why dost thou set at nought thy brother. . .Let us not therefore judge one another any more. . . (Romans 14:10 and 13)**

LIMIT LIBERTY BY LOVE:

The basic message of Romans 14:13-15:2 is that Christian liberty should be limited by love:

> **Let every one of us please his neighbor for his good to edification. (Romans 15:2)**

You should care for other believers so much that you limit your own behavior by love for them. You should love them so much that you will not do anything that would cause them to stumble spiritually:

> **. . .but judge this rather, that no man put a stumbling block or an occasion to fall in his brother's way. (Romans 14:13)**

RESOLVE ALL OFFENSES:

When a brother has been offended by another believer, Matthew 18:15-17 provides the Biblical formula for resolving such offenses:

> **Moreover if thy brother shall trespass against thee, go and tell him his fault between thee and him alone: If he shall hear thee, thou hast gained thy brother.**
>
> **But if he will not hear thee, then take with thee one or two more, that in the mouth of two or three witnesses every word may be established.**
>
> **And if he shall neglect to hear them, tell it unto the church; but if he neglect to hear the church, let him be unto thee as an heathen man and a publican. (Matthew 18:15-17)**

The steps to follow when a brother has offended you are:

1.   Go to him privately to resolve the matter. Do not talk about the offense to others. Go directly to the one who offended you and try to resolve the matter. Pray and search God's written Word together.

2.   If he will not listen to you, take one or two witnesses and try again. The witnesses should be impartial believers. Elders or leaders in the church would be a good choice. Take the witnesses and go to your brother and again attempt to discuss, pray, and search the Scriptures together regarding the problem.

3.   Take the matter before the entire church body. If, after going to your brother with a witness he still refuses to resolve the matter, take the issue before the entire church body. This should be done at the proper time. It should not be done during a regular worship service or when unbelievers are present. After hearing the matter, the decision of the church should be abided by and the problem should be resolved. If not, then the offending party is acting like the heathen and unbelievers.

SUMMARY: WHEN BELIEVERS DIFFER

The following chart summarizes Scriptural guidelines to follow when believers differ in regards to questionable practices:

When Believers Differ
Romans 14-15:2 and Matthew 18:15-17

Distinguish between matters of command and freedom.
Cultivate your own convictions.
Allow others freedom to determine their own convictions.
Limit liberty by love.
Resolve all offenses.

SELF-TEST

1.   Write the Key Verse from memory.

_____

_____

2.   What is meant by the term "questionable practices"?

_____

3.   List ten Biblical guidelines given in this chapter for dealing with questionable practices:

_____ _____ _____ _____ _____

_____ _____ _____ _____ _____

4.   What is meant by the term a "weaker brother"?

_____

5.   What is meant by a "stronger brother"?

_____

6.   List five Biblical guidelines for handling disagreements between believers:

_____   _____

_____   _____

_____

7.   What are three steps to take when you have been offended by another believer?

_____   _____   _____

(Answers to tests are provided at the conclusion of the final chapter in this manual.)

FOR FURTHER STUDY

Prayerfully examine your own life. Make a list of questionable practices in which you are currently engaging or considering.

Examine each of these in terms of the Biblical guidelines given in this chapter which are summarized on the following chart:

DECISION MAKING ON QUESTIONABLE PRACTICES

Ask Yourself. . .	Biblical Reference
Does it glorify God?	I Corinthians 10:31; Colossians 3:17,23
What is your motivation?	James 4:3
Is it necessary?	I Corinthians 6:12
Will it promote spiritual growth?	Mark 4:18,19; Luke 8:14; Hebrews 12:1
Is it an enslaving habit?	I Corinthians 6:12
Is it a compromise?	II Corinthians 6:17
Will it lead to temptation?	James 1:13-15
Does it give the appearance of evil?	I Thessalonians 5:22
Does it violate your conscience?	Romans 14:23
How will it affect others?	Romans 14:19,21; I Corinthians 8:13; 10:23

CHAPTER NINE

A BIBLICAL MODEL FOR DECISION MAKING

OBJECTIVES:

Upon completion of this chapter you will be able to:

- Write the Key Verse from memory.
- Explain the purpose of a model.
- Explain the value of a model for decision making.
- Use a Biblical model for decision making to help you make wise choices.

KEY VERSE:

> **A man's heart deviseth his way; but the Lord directeth his steps.**
> **(Proverbs 16:9)**

INTRODUCTION

This chapter presents a Biblical model for decision making. A model is an example of something. Its purpose is to provide an example for you to follow. A decision is a choice. You must determine an answer for a real life situation and choose what action you will take. This is called decision making. A model for decision making provides an example to follow when making decisions. Life is an endless succession of choices and decisions. Making choices is a responsibility. Constantly refusing to make a decision is in itself a decision.

The Biblical model presented in this chapter will help you make wise choices within the will of God:

> **A man's heart deviseth his way; but the Lord directeth his steps.**
> **(Proverbs 16:9)**

THE MODEL

Study the Biblical model for decision making on the following page. The chart summarizes what you have learned in previous chapters. Then proceed on to discussion of the model in the remainder of this chapter.

A BIBLICAL MODEL FOR DECISION MAKING

Identify the problem, question, or life situation for which guidance is sought.

Is it dealt with in Scripture by specific command, general principle or example?

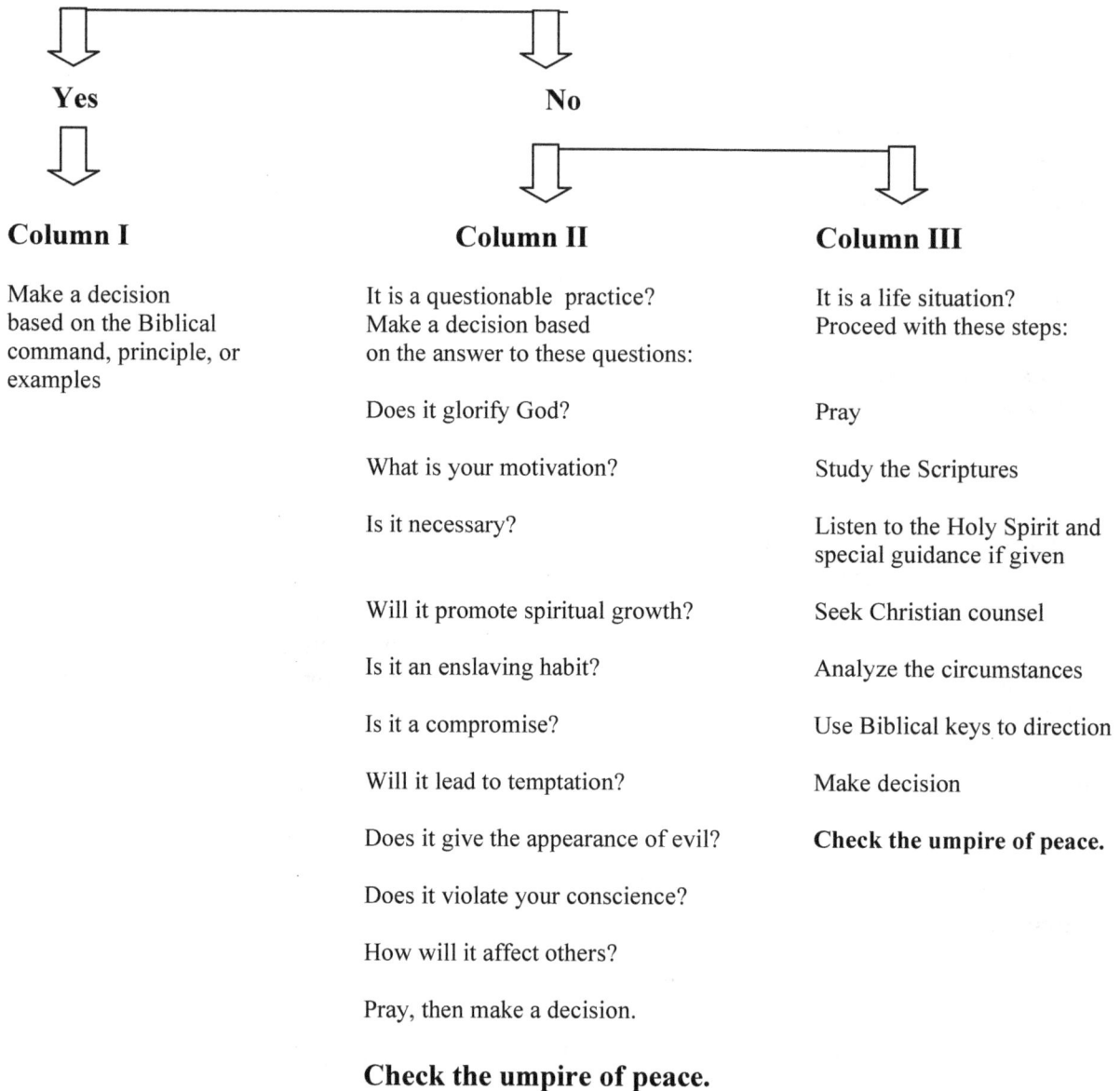

Yes

No

Column I

Make a decision based on the Biblical command, principle, or examples

Column II

It is a questionable practice? Make a decision based on the answer to these questions:

Does it glorify God?

What is your motivation?

Is it necessary?

Will it promote spiritual growth?

Is it an enslaving habit?

Is it a compromise?

Will it lead to temptation?

Does it give the appearance of evil?

Does it violate your conscience?

How will it affect others?

Pray, then make a decision.

Check the umpire of peace.

Column III

It is a life situation? Proceed with these steps:

Pray

Study the Scriptures

Listen to the Holy Spirit and special guidance if given

Seek Christian counsel

Analyze the circumstances

Use Biblical keys to direction

Make decision

Check the umpire of peace.

If you do not have peace, continue to seek the Lord using the model.

USING THE MODEL

The first step in the decision making model is to identify the problem, question, or life situation for which guidance is sought. Next, search the written Word of God to see if the problem is dealt with by commandment, example, or general principle.

YES:

If the answer is "Yes, it is dealt with in the written Word of God," then make the decision based upon this written revelation. (See Column I on the model). Make sure your decision is in harmony with the Scriptures.

NO:

If the answer is "no," then proceed on with the decision making model under Columns I and II.

Here you will find two choices for situations not dealt with in the Bible. You must determine whether the decision to be made involves a questionable practice or a real life situation.

QUESTIONABLE PRACTICES:

A questionable practice is something not dealt with in Scripture as either right or wrong. It can involve a choice of entertainment or leisure activities, a habit, permissible food or drinks, style of dress, or day on which to worship.

If the decision with which you are faced involves a questionable practice, ask yourself the questions listed on the model under Column II. These are Biblical principles for guidance in questionable situations which were discussed in Chapter Eight. Answer each of these questions and pray, then make your decision on the basis of your answers to the questions on the model.

LIFE SITUATIONS:

A life situation can include, but is not limited to, decisions regarding marriage, ministry, occupation, residence, choice of churches, etc. It is a choice which can affect your future life in a major way.

For decisions on life issues, proceed down Column III on the right hand side of the decision making model. First pray about the decision. Ask God for His will to be accomplished in your life. Ask Him for wisdom to make the right decision. Praise Him for guidance to make the right decision. Ask others to pray with you. Study the Scriptures and as you study claim the promises for direction given in the written Word of God.

Listen to the inner voice of the Holy Spirit as He speaks God's will into your heart. Acknowledge supernatural revelation, should God choose to send it. These might include dreams, visions, angels, an audible voice from God, or other special forms of guidance in harmony with God's Word.

Seek Christian counsel. Analyze the circumstances affecting the decision. Use the Biblical keys for direction you learned in the last chapter. (These are found in Proverbs 3:5-6). On the basis of agreement of these methods, make a decision.

THE UMPIRE OF PEACE

On decisions not specifically dealt with by Biblical command, principle, or example, the umpire of peace is your guide. When you make a decision on a questionable practice or life situation and you do not have peace in your spirit, continue to seek the Lord using the steps on the model. Do not make a final decision until you have the peace of God confirming your choice.

Never be in a hurry:

> **Wait on the Lord; be of good courage, and He shall strengthen thine heart: wait, I say, on the Lord. (Psalms 27:14)**

> **My soul, wait thou only upon God; for my expectation is from him. (Psalms 62:5)**

> **Rest in the Lord, and wait patiently for Him . . . (Psalms 37:7)**

> **But they that wait upon the Lord shall renew their strength; they shall mount up with wings as eagles; they shall run, and not be weary; and they shall walk, and not faint. (Isaiah 40:31)**

Saul was in a hurry and made a decision which cost him the kingdom. You can read about it in I Samuel 13. Nehemiah waited for direction from God and the right timing, and he became part of the rebuilding of a kingdom. You can read his story in the book of Nehemiah.

SELF-TEST

1.   Write the Key Verse from memory.

_____

_____

2.   What is the purpose of a model?

_____

_____

_____

_____

3.   What is a model for decision making?

_____

_____

_____

_____

(Answers to tests are provided at the conclusion of the final chapter in this manual.)

FOR FURTHER STUDY

Use the Biblical model presented in this chapter to help you make a decision about a problem, question, or life situation for which you need guidance.

CHAPTER TEN

TRIED AND FAILED?

OBJECTIVES:

Upon completion of this chapter you will be able to:

- Write the Key Verse from memory.
- Identify Biblical examples of men who overcame failure to return to the perfect will of God.
- Identify Biblical examples of men who missed the will of God and their lives ended in failure.
- List guidelines for getting back into God's will when you fail.

KEY VERSE:

> **Oh, that my people had hearkened unto me and Israel had walked in my ways. (Psalms 81:13)**

INTRODUCTION

In this course you learned many ways God speaks to man to communicate His will. But what happens when you fail to discern the will of God? Perhaps you deliberately disobey His voice. Perhaps you miss His direction through error or misunderstanding of Biblical principles. Maybe you act too quickly without His guidance. What should you do when you have tried and failed?

FAILURES WHO WERE SUCCESSES

The Bible contains many examples of great leaders who at some point in their lives failed to listen to the voice of God and missed His will. Yet, these men who failed became great successes:

Abraham: He lied about Sarah being his wife for fear he would be killed and his wife taken from him. Yet he is called a man of faith and the friend of God.

Moses: He struck the rock and called forth water instead of speaking to it as God directed. Yet the Bible states there has never been another prophet as great as Moses.

David: He committed adultery with another man's wife, then had the man killed to try to cover his sin. Yet he was a great king and is called a man after God's own heart.

Jonah: This preacher went the opposite direction when God called him to preach in Ninevah. Later he preached the greatest revival in history. The whole city repented.

Peter: He denied Jesus, but later became a great leader in the early church.

FAILURES WHO WERE FAILURES

The Bible also contains many examples of men who missed the will of God and their lives ended in failure and defeat:

Samson: He was an important judge in the nation of Israel and had great physical strength given him from God. He began to deliver Israel from the Philistine enemy. But through involvement with a heathen woman, Samson was taken captive and died while yet a prisoner of the enemy.

Uziah: This king originally did what was right in the sight of the Lord and God made him prosper. But Uziah sinned by entering the temple and performing duties which only the priests were permitted to do. He was stricken with leprosy and died.

Saul: The first king of Israel, Saul was a man adored by the people and upon whom the Spirit of God rested. Because of disobedience, Saul was rejected by God and another king was selected to complete his task. Saul's life ended in failure, disgrace, and suicide.

Eli: Originally a great priest in the house of the Lord, Eli and his sons died in disgrace because of disobedience.

Judas: Judas was a disciple of Jesus during His earthly ministry. He witnessed the great miracles of Jesus and heard His teachings. Yet he betrayed Jesus and ended his own life by suicide.

WHAT MADE THE DIFFERENCE?

We have listed several Biblical examples of men who at some point in their lives failed to discern God's will. Some of these men recovered from failure and went on to be great men of God. Others never reversed their direction. Their lives ended in failure. What made the difference?

To answer this question, let us examine in more detail the lives of two kings of Israel, David and Saul. First, read the story of David's departure from God's will in II Samuel chapters 11-12. Then read the story of Saul's failure in I Samuel chapter 15. David's failure appears so much greater than that of Saul. Saul simply brought back some oxen as spoil from battle when God had told him not to do so.

David committed adultery with another man's wife. When she became pregnant he had her husband killed to try to cover the sin. Saul was rejected by God as king, yet David remained on the throne and was called a man after God's own heart. Why did one man's life end in failure while the other went on to future successes?

When the prophet Samuel confronted Saul with his sin, Saul said. . .

> **. . .I have sinned: for I have transgressed the commandment of the Lord, and thy words: because I feared the people, and obeyed their voice.**

> **Then he said, I have sinned; yet honor me now, I pray thee, before the elders of my people and before Israel, and turn again with me, that I worship the Lord thy God.   (I Samuel 15:24 and 30)**

Saul was caught in his sin and he admitted it. He was sorry, but only for being caught. Being sorry for sin is not enough. Sorrow must lead to repentance:

> **For godly sorrow worketh repentance to salvation not to be repented of: but the sorrow of the world worketh death. (II Corinthians 7:10)**

Saul admitted he failed, but he blamed his failure on other people. He wanted Samuel to honor him before the leaders so he would not be disgraced. He wanted Samuel to worship God with him to show people he was still a spiritual man.

Saul never confessed his sin to God, repented, and asked forgiveness. He refused to accept personal responsibility for his actions. He offered God worship when God wanted repentance. Saul was more concerned about his reputation among the people than his relationship to God. Because of this, Samuel told Saul:

> **. . .The Lord hath rent the kingdom of Israel from thee this day, and hath given it to a neighbor of thine, that is better than thou. (I Samuel 15:28)**

The kingdom was taken from Saul and given to David.

When the prophet Nathan confronted David about his sin, David immediately acknowledged:

> **I have sinned against the Lord. (II Samuel 12:13)**

He did not try to blame others. He did not blame Bathsheba. He admitted his failure and humbly repented before God.

David's great prayer of repentance is recorded in Psalms 51. Read this entire Psalm in your Bible. David acknowledged his sin and asked forgiveness:

For I acknowledge my transgressions: and my sin is ever before me.

Against thee, thee only have I sinned and done this evil in thy sight. . .

Create in me a clean heart O God; and renew a right spirit within me. (Portions of Psalms 51

Both Saul and David made wrong choices. When confronted with his error, David repented and changed direction. Saul did not. He strayed farther from the will of God and his life ended in failure, defeat, and suicide.

TRIED AND FAILED?

When you have missed the will of God, there are Biblical guidelines which will enable you to return to the will of the Lord. To illustrate these guidelines we will use the example of Jonah. Read the book of Jonah in your Bible before proceeding with this lesson.

Jonah was commanded by the Lord to go and preach repentance to the sinful nation of Ninevah. Instead of obeying God, he headed the opposite direction. Jonah took the following steps to return to the will of God. These are steps to take when you experience failure:

REALIZE YOUR FAILURE:

It took a great storm at sea to convince Jonah he was out of the will of God. (Jonah 1:2) Be assured: God has ways of letting you know when you have missed His will!

As long as you fail to realize you have missed the will of God, you can never get back into His will. Do not let any excuse prevent you from admitting failure. Here are some common ones:

> "People will lose confidence in me."
> "If I admit failure it is admitting I was wrong."
> "I already failed. I might as well give up."
> "It is too late."
> "I am a bad example, so I should just quit."
> "I am too far out of the will of God to ever get things right."
> "I don't know if I can even find the will of God again."

REPENT OF YOUR SIN:

Jonah's great prayer of repentance is recorded in Jonah chapter 2. Jonah acknowledged his sin before God, repented, and asked forgiveness. When you miss the will of God, come before the Lord in repentance and ask God to forgive you. Be sure to forgive yourself, too! It is not necessary to repent publicly unless it has affected the lives of others and you need to ask their forgiveness. It is necessary to repent before God.

110

RECOGNIZE THE DEPARTURE POINT:

Through prayer, the written Word of God, and the guidance of the Holy Spirit, determine the point at which you missed God's will. In the case of Jonah, he recognized his departure from the will of God began when he went the opposite direction from Ninevah.

RETURN TO CORRECT THE ERROR:

Return to the point of departure and correct the error, if possible. When Jonah recognized his failure began by heading the opposite direction from Ninevah, he reversed directions. He went to Ninevah. He corrected his error (Jonah 3:3).

Sometimes you can do nothing to correct an error except repent. In the example of David which we discussed, he could do nothing about his sin with Bathsheba after it was committed. The mistake was already made. There was nothing he could do to correct it except repent. In situations where you can take corrective action, however, it should be done.

REVELATION. . .SEEK GOD FOR AND ACT UPON NEW DIRECTION:

After you admit your failure, ask forgiveness, determine the point of departure, and correct any errors possible, seek the Lord for new direction. Remove any hindrances to hearing the voice of God. These might include sins of rebellion, self-will, and wrong attitudes. Continue to train your spiritual ear to hear God's voice by praying and studying His written Word.
As Jonah sought God for new direction, the Lord spoke unto him a second time and said, "Arise, and go to Ninevah" (Jonah 3:1-2). This time, Jonah obeyed the voice of the Lord. He went to Ninevah and preached the message of God. He experienced the greatest revival in history. The whole city repented (Jonah chapter 3).

The Bible contains many stories of men like Jonah. These men failed but admitted their failure and asked forgiveness. When they did, God always forgave them and provided new direction. He will do the same for you! God is not looking at your past record. He is not looking at you as you are. He is seeing the man or woman you can be if you walk in obedience to the voice of God.

SUMMARY

The following chart summarizes Biblical guidelines to follow when you miss the will of God:

WHEN YOU MISS GOD'S WILL

Recognize Your Failure

Repent Of Your Sin

Recognize The Departure Point

Return To Correct The Error

Revelation: Seek God For And Act Upon New Direction

SELF-TEST

1. Write the Key Verse from memory.

    _____

    _____

    _____

2. Identify three Biblical examples great men who triumphed over their failures and returned to the perfect will of God.

    _____

    _____

    _____

3. Identify three Biblical examples of men who missed the will of God and whose lives ended in failure:

    _____

    _____

    _____

4. List five guidelines for getting back into God's will when you have failed:

    _____   _____

    _____   _____

    _____

(Answers to tests are provided at the conclusion of the final chapter in this manual.)

FOR FURTHER STUDY

1. In Luke 15:11-32 Jesus told the story of a young man who left his father and went to live in a strange country. Study this story carefully, especially the portion which tells of the son's return to the house of his father. You will discover he followed the guidelines for correcting failure which were discussed in this chapter.

2. Study the following examples of men who at some point in their lives missed the will of God. Which ones corrected their failures? How did they turn their failures into success? Which ones did not correct their failures? What was the result?

   Abraham: Genesis 20-21
   Moses: Exodus; see also Acts 7:20-44
   Balaam: Numbers 22
   Uziah: II Chronicles 26
   Samson: Judges 13-16
   David: II Samuel 11-12; Psalms 51.
   Saul: I Samuel 8-15
   Jonah: The book of Jonah
   Peter: Matthew, Mark, Luke, John, Acts
   John Mark: Acts 12:12, 25; 15:39; II Timothy 4:11

   You can add other examples to this list from your own study of God's Word.

3. Jesus told two important parables about the will of God. Study Luke 12:42-48 and Matthew 21:28-32 and summarize what you learn.

_____

_____

_____

_____

CHAPTER ELEVEN

GOD'S WILL AND SUFFERING

OBJECTIVES:

Upon completion of this chapter you will be able to:

- Write the Key Verse from memory.
- Identify five reasons for suffering.
- Recognize that the will of God may entail suffering.
- Distinguish between suffering within and without of the will of God.
- List positive benefits of suffering within the will of God.

KEY VERSE:

Wherefore let them that suffer according to the will of God, commit the keeping of their souls to Him in well doing as unto a faithful creator. (I Peter 4:19)

INTRODUCTION

You heard the voice of God. You sought guidance, it was given, and you set off along the road of life which God seemed to indicate. But as a result of this decision you are experiencing problems which would not have arisen apart from this new path of "God's will" on which you travel.

Did you really hear the voice of God or have you made a mistake? Are these difficult experiences a sign from God that you are not living in His will? Does God permit suffering to come to someone who is living righteously within the will of God?

When Jesus was here on earth and spoke of the suffering He was to face on the cross, many of His followers deserted Him (John 6:55-66). They expected the Messiah to reign in power and glory. Instead, He spoke of suffering. They could not understand, so they turned away.

If you do not understand suffering as it relates to the will of God, then you too may turn from following Jesus when you face difficult circumstances. God did not create suffering. It originally entered the world through man's sin (Genesis 3). But God can take that which is intended for evil and use it for good to accomplish His purposes.

THE REASONS FOR SUFFERING

The Bible has much to say concerning suffering, problems, and afflictions. In summarizing its teaching, we discover five ways suffering can come into the life of a believer:

OTHERS AROUND YOU:

Suffering may come through others around you. Joseph is an example of this type of suffering. Through no fault of his own, Joseph was sold into Egypt by his brothers, imprisoned falsely by Potiphar's wife, and forgotten by those he helped in prison.

But listen to his response. Joseph said. . .

> **Now therefore be not grieved, nor angry with yourselves, that ye sold me hither; for God did send me before you to preserve life. . .so now it was not you that sent me hither but God. (Genesis 45:5,7)**

CIRCUMSTANCES OF LIFE:

The second way suffering comes is through the circumstances of life. This is illustrated by the example of Naomi, recorded in the book of Ruth in the Bible, who experienced the death of her husband and sons.

Until Jesus returns and the final enemy of death is conquered, death is part of life. Death entered through the original sin of man and it is a natural circumstance which we all will face, because "it is appointed unto man once to die" (Hebrews 9:27).

YOUR MINISTRY:

The third reason for suffering is because of your ministry for the Lord. The New Testament speaks of suffering for His name's sake (Acts 9:16), in behalf of Christ, (Philippians 1:29) for the Kingdom of God (II Thessalonians 1:5), for the Gospel (II Timothy 1:11-12), for well-doing (I Peter 2:19-20; 3:17), for righteousness sake (I Peter 3:14), as a Christian (I Peter 4:15-16), and according to the will of God (I Peter 4:19).

The Apostle Paul is an example of suffering resulting from ministry. Some people view suffering as a sign of failure or lack of faith. If this is true, then the Apostle Paul had no faith and was the greatest failure in the history of the church.

Paul said that while in Asia he was so utterly crushed that he despaired of life itself (II Corinthians 1:8). He presents a different image than that of the cheerful evangelist who promises believers nothing but peace and prosperity. When Paul was first called of God to ministry he was told of "great things" he would suffer for the sake of the Lord (Acts 9:16).

Paul's response to suffering was to endure "the loss of all things to win some for Christ." He wrote to believers "to you it is given not only to believe, but to suffer for Him" (Philippians 1:29).

Paul was not alone in suffering for the ministry. The whole church suffered in New Testament times (Acts 8). Hebrews chapter 11 records the stories some of the cruel persecutions they endured. Many of these men and women of faith were delivered by the power of God. Prison doors were opened and they walked out. They were sentenced to death in fiery furnaces but emerged unaffected by the flames.

But some of these believers, who are also called men and women of faith, did not receive deliverance. They were imprisoned, afflicted, tormented, and even martyred because of their testimony of the Gospel (Hebrews 11:36-40). We focus on living faith but God also reveals His power in dying faith. This is a faith that stands true in the bad times, not just in good times when mighty deliverances are manifested.

DIRECT SATANIC ACTIVITY:

Suffering can also enter your life as a result of direct Satanic activity. This is evident in the story of Job. This book wrestles with the question, "Why do the righteous suffer?"

God's testimony of Job was that he was a righteous man (Job 1-2). Job did not suffer because he sinned, as his friends claimed. They believed if Job repented, his circumstances would change. These friends tried to make a universal application based on individual experience. It would be similar to saying that because God delivered Peter from prison He will do the same for you. This is not true. Many have been martyred in prison despite their great faith and sinless lives.

We must be careful when we view the suffering of others that we do not accuse them of sin, faithlessness, or unbelief. The Bible does teach that a sinful man reaps a bitter harvest because of sowing in fleshly corruption (Galatians 6:8). But sowing and reaping cannot be used to explain the suffering of the innocent.

Job did not suffer because of anything he did. He was a righteous man. This was God's testimony of Job, Job's testimony of himself, and his reputation before man. Behind the scenes in the spiritual world was the true cause of Job's suffering. There was a spiritual battle going on over the heart, mind, and allegiance of Job.

There is warfare going on in the spiritual world over you. That warfare is manifested in the difficult circumstances you experience in the natural world. An important truth evident in Job's suffering is that nothing can enter the life of a believer without the knowledge of God. God does not cause your suffering. It is inflicted by Satan, but its limits are set by God.

YOUR OWN SIN:

The fifth way suffering enters your life is because of your own sin. Jonah is an example of such suffering. In disobedience to God, Jonah headed the opposite direction from Ninevah where he was told to go and preach repentance. He experienced a terrible storm at sea and ended up in the belly of a great fish because of his own sin (Jonah 1-2).

Trouble should always be treated as a call to consider your ways and examine your heart before God. Like Jonah, you may be suffering because of your own sin. The Bible reveals that God chastises those who live in disobedience to His Word. Chastise means to discipline, reprove, and correct:

> **Now no chastening for the present seemeth to be joyous, but grievous: nevertheless afterward it yieldeth the peaceable fruit of righteousness unto them which are exercised thereby. (Hebrews 12:11)**

God uses suffering to correct you and bring you back to His will for your life:

> **Before I was afflicted I went astray; but now have I kept thy Word. . .**

> **It is good for me that I have been afflicted; that I might learn thy statutes.**

> **I know, O Lord, that thy judgments are right, and that THOU in faithfulness hast afflicted me. (Psalms 119:67,71,75)**

THE PROPER ATTITUDE TOWARDS SUFFERING

But trouble is not necessarily a sign of being out of God's will. The Bible declares that "many are the afflictions of the righteous" (Psalms 34:19). When you suffer innocently and not because of your own sin, you should maintain a proper attitude towards suffering. The real test of your spirituality is how you respond in the day of distress:

> **If thou faint in the day of adversity, thy strength is small. (Proverbs 24:10)**

The Bible describes the attitude you should have when you suffer as a believer within the will of God. You should not be ashamed:

> **If any man suffer as a Christian let him not be ashamed, but let him glorify God on this behalf. . .(I Peter 4:16)**

You should commit your soul (your suffering) to God, knowing He works all things for your good:

Wherefore let them that suffer according to the will of God commit the keeping of their souls to Him in well doing as unto a faithful Creator. (I Peter 4:19)

You should be happy when you suffer according to the will of God:

And they departed from the presence of the council, rejoicing that they were counted worthy to suffer shame for His name. (Acts 5:41)

Paul says you should be:

Rejoicing in hope; patient in tribulation; continuing instant in prayer. (Romans 12:12)

. . .being reviled, we bless; being persecuted, we suffer it. . . (I Corinthians 4:12)

. . .in all things approving ourselves as the ministers of God, in much patience, in afflictions, in necessities, in distresses. . . (II Corinthians 6:4)

. . . be thou partaker of the afflictions of the gospel according to the power of God. (II Timothy 1:8)

That no man should be moved by these afflictions: for yourselves know that we are appointed thereunto. (I Thessalonians 3:3)

But watch thou in all things, endure afflictions, do the work of an evangelist, make full proof of thy ministry. (II Timothy 4:5)

You should not think it strange when you experience suffering:

Beloved, think it not strange concerning the fiery trial which is to try you, as though some strange thing happened unto you; but rejoice, inasmuch as ye are partaker of Christ's sufferings; that when His glory shall be revealed ye may be glad with exceeding joy. (I Peter 4:12-13)

You are to endure hardness like a soldier:

Thou therefore endure hardness as a good soldier of Jesus Christ. (II Timothy 2:3)

Paul summarizes the proper attitude toward suffering in II Corinthians 4:9:

> . . .though our outward man perish, yet the inward man is renewed day by day.
>
> For our light affliction, which is but for a moment, worketh for us a far more exceeding and eternal weight of glory:
>
> While we look not at the things which are seen, but at the things which are not seen: for the things which are seen are temporal; but the things which are not seen are eternal. . . (II Corinthians 4:16-18)

Paul viewed suffering as a servant. He said it works for us when w keep our eyes on its eternal benefits instead of the problem.

POSITIVE BENEFITS OF SUFFERING

Here are some positive benefits of suffering according to God's will:

YOUR FAITH IS TESTED:

Everything in the spiritual world is based on faith. This is why the strength of your faith must be tested:

> That the trial of your faith being much more precious than of gold that perisheth though it be tried with fire, might be found unto praise and honour and glory at the appearing of Jesus Christ. (I Peter 1:7)

It is a trial of faith when you pray as Jesus did, for God to let the cup of bitterness pass, and yet it does not pass. Instead, you are forced to drink deeply of its suffering. But faith will learn that our prayers are not unanswered just because they are not answered the way we want.

YOU ARE ABLE TO COMFORT OTHERS:

> Blessed be God, even the Father of our Lord Jesus Christ, the Father of mercies, and the God of all comfort;
>
> Who comforteth us in all our tribulation that we may be able to comfort them which are in any trouble, by the comfort wherewith we ourselves are comforted of God. (II Corinthians 1:3-4)

When you share God's comfort with others you. . .

> . . .lift up the hands which hang down, and the feeble knees;

And make straight paths for your feet, lest that which is lame be turned out of the way; but let it rather be healed. (Hebrews 12:12-13)

YOU LEARN NOT TO TRUST YOUR OWN SELF:

Paul spoke of the purpose of his sufferings in Asia:

. . .In Asia we were pressed out of measure, above strength, insomuch that we despaired even of life;

But we had the sentence of death in ourselves, that we should not trust in ourselves but in God which raiseth the dead. (II Corinthians 1:8-9)

You will come to recognize that. . .

. . . we have this treasure in earthen vessels, that the excellency of the power may be of God, and not of us. (II Corinthians 4:7)

POSITIVE QUALITIES ARE DEVELOPED:

We glory in tribulations, knowing that tribulation worketh patience, and patience experience, and experience hope, (resulting in the love of God being shed abroad in our hearts). (Romans 5:3-4)

. . .after ye have suffered awhile, make you perfect, stablish, strengthen, settle you. (I Peter 5:10)

These qualities conform you to the image of Jesus, which is God's plan for you (Romans 8:28-29; Hebrews 2:10,18).

THE WORKS OF GOD ARE MANIFESTED:

When the disciples saw a man who had been blind from birth, they asked who was responsible for his condition. Was it the sin of his parents or of the man himself? Jesus answered:

Neither this man sinned nor His parents; but that the works of God should be made manifest in Him. (John 9:3)

THE POWER OF GOD IS PERFECTED:

And He said unto me, My grace is sufficient for thee; for my strength is made perfect in weakness. Most gladly therefore will I rather glory in my infirmities, that the power of Christ may rest upon me. (II Corinthians 12:9)

THAT WHICH IS UNSTABLE IS REMOVED:

Suffering results in all that is unstable being shaken out of your life. You cease to depend on people, programs, or material things because these all fail in your time of need.

God permits this. . .

> **. . .removing of those things that are shaken as of things that are made, that those things which cannot be shaken may remain.**
> **(Hebrews 12:26-27)**

During the storms of life, everything crumbles that is not built upon God and His Word (Psalm 119:89 and Matthew 7:24-27).

YOUR FOCUS IS CHANGED:

When you experience suffering you often focus your attention on cause and effect. You are concerned with what caused the difficult circumstances and the terrible effect it is having in your life. God wants to change your focus from the temporal to the eternal:

> **For our light affliction, which is but for a moment, worketh for us a far more exceeding and eternal weight of glory;**
>
> **While we look not at the things which are seen, but at the things which are not seen; for the things which are seen are temporal; but the things which are not seen are eternal. (II Corinthians 4:17-18)**
>
> **Beloved, think it not strange concerning the fiery trial which is to try you, as though some strange thing happened unto you:**
>
> **But rejoice, inasmuch as ye are partakers of Christ's sufferings; that, when His glory shall be revealed, ye may be glad also with exceeding joy. (I Peter 4:12-13)**
>
> **If we suffer, we shall also reign with Him. . . (II Timothy 2:12)**

THE OLD SELF-NATURE IS CHANGED:

God said of the nation of Moab:

> **Moab hath been at ease from his youth, and he hath settled on his lees, and hath not been emptied from vessel to vessel, neither hath he gone into captivity; therefore his taste remained in him, and his scent is not changed. (Jeremiah 48:11)**

122

Because Moab had not experienced the troublesome pouring out and stirring similar to that necessary to develop good wine, the nation did not change. Because Moab was at ease and settled in prosperity the nation did not develop and mature spiritually. Therefore there was no change. His own scent remained in him.

Suffering rids you of the old self-nature. As you are stirred, troubled, and poured out, your spiritual scent changes from carnal to spiritual.

GOD PREPARES YOU FOR MINISTRY:

You want to be used by God. You desire to be more like Jesus and be a chosen vessel for His use. God answers your prayer through suffering:

> **Behold I have refined thee, but not with silver; I have chosen thee in the furnace of affliction. (Isaiah 48:10)**

It is through affliction that you move beyond the calling as a child of God to become chosen of God. Affliction according to the will of God refines you for His use just as metals are refined in a furnace in the natural world.

YOU ARE PREPARED TO REIGN WITH CHRIST:

> **If we suffer, we shall also reign with Him. . .(II Timothy 2:12)**

SUFFERING BRINGS SPIRITUAL BLESSING:

Jesus said:

> **Blessed are they which are persecuted for righteousness sake; for theirs is the Kingdom of Heaven.**
>
> **Blessed are ye, when men shall revile you, and persecute you, and shall say all manner of evil against you falsely, for my sake.**
>
> **Rejoice, and be exceeding glad: for great is your reward in heaven: for so persecuted they the prophets which were before you. (Matthew 5:10-12)**

YOU LEARN OBEDIENCE THROUGH SUFFERING:

> **Though He were a Son, yet learned He obedience by the things which He suffered. . . (Hebrews 5:8)**

SUFFERING TESTS THE WORD OF GOD WITHIN YOU:

> **The words of the Lord are pure words: as silver tried in a furnace of earth, purified seven times. (Psalms 12:6)**

SUFFERING HUMBLES YOU:

> **Who led thee through that great and terrible wilderness, wherein were fiery serpents, and scorpions, and drought, where there was no water; who brought thee forth water out of the rock of flint;**
>
> **Who fed thee in the wilderness with manna, which thy fathers knew not, that He might humble thee, and that He might prove thee, to do thee good at thy latter end. . . (Deuteronomy 8:15-16)**

SUFFERING ENLARGES YOU:

This means you grow spiritually:

> **Thou has enlarged me when I was under pressure.**
> **(Psalms 4:1 Revised Standard Version)**

YOU COME TO KNOW GOD INTIMATELY:

You come to know God on a more intimate basis through suffering. Job, who suffered much, learned this truth and said. . .

> **I have heard of thee by the hearing of the ear: but now mine eye seeth thee.**
>
> **Wherefore I abhor myself and repent in dust and ashes. (Job 42:5-6)**

Some of us know God only second handedly. When you are experiencing the blessings of life, God is often a luxury instead of a necessity. But when you have a real need, God becomes a necessity. Job came to know God more intimately through suffering. Before he suffered, Job knew God through theology. Afterwards, he knew Him by experience.

Paul expressed a similar desire when he said:

> **That I may know Him, and the power of His resurrection and the fellowship of His sufferings, being made conformable unto His death.**
> **(Philippians 3:10)**

You can only come to know God in resurrection power through the intimate fellowship of suffering.

Throughout his trial, Job questioned God as to the cause of his suffering. It is not wrong to question God. Jesus knew the purpose for which He had come into the world was to die for the sins of all mankind. Yet in His hour of suffering He cried out, "My God, My God, WHY hast thou forsaken me?" It is what follows the questioning that is important. Jesus's next words were, "Into thy hands I commit my spirit."

Despite the questions, Job's response was. . .

> **Though He slay me, yet will I trust in Him. . .(Job 13:15)**

> **For I know that my Redeemer liveth, and that He shall stand at the latter day upon the earth:**

> **And though after my skin worms destroy this body, yet in my flesh shall I see God. (Job 19:25-26)**

After all the questioning is finished, the emphasis must change from "me" to "Thee." You must commit your suffering, with all its unanswered questions, into the hands of God.

> **Trust in the Lord with all thine heart; and lean not unto thine own understanding. (Proverbs 3:5)**

God may reveal some of the purposes in your suffering, but it is possible you will never fully understand it:

> **It is the glory of God to conceal a thing. . .(Proverbs 25:2)**

> **The secret things belong unto the Lord our God; but those things which are revealed belong unto us. . . (Deuteronomy 29:29)**

There are some secret things that belong only to the Lord. As Job, you may never understand all the purposes of your suffering:

> **Since the Lord is directing our steps, why try to understand everything that happens along the way? (Proverbs 20:24, The Living Bible)**

When God finally talked with Job, He used several examples from nature which Job could not explain. God stressed that if Job could not understand what he saw in the natural world, he certainly could not understand that which he could not see in the spiritual world.

When Job faced God, it no longer mattered that he did not get an answer to his questions about suffering. He was no longer controlled and tormented by human reasoning. He replaced questions, not with answers, but with faith.

When you come to know God intimately through suffering, you see yourself as you really are. You no longer know God second-handedly. That face-to-face encounter with God does what arguments and discussions cannot do.

When Job stood before God, he had no new answers. He was given no new facts about his suffering. But he replaced questions with faith. Job had been in the direct presence of God, and that experience left no room for questions or doubts.

THE STORMS OF LIFE

Suffering is sometimes compared to a natural storm. When you suffer, you experience a storm spiritually speaking. This storm may affect you spiritually, mentally, physically, materially, or emotionally.

The Bible tells of a storm which the disciples of Jesus experienced. Read the story in your Bible in Mark 4:35-41. This storm was an attack of Satan. Jesus had told the disciples to go to the other side. Jesus was with them in the boat. Satan was trying to prevent them from reaching the shore because of the miraculous works that were to be done in the country of the Gadarenes (Mark 5). Jesus took authority over the storm. He rebuked the powers of the enemy. Calm returned to the sea and they continued their journey unhindered.

A storm of Satan is anything that tries to hinder you from fulfilling the will of God for your life. It is not suffering resulting from your disobedience. Neither is this kind of suffering according to the will of God. God does not want anything to hinder His plan for you. When you face this type of storm, exercise authority over the enemy. Jesus has given you power over every power of Satan.

There are two other stories of natural storms recorded in the Bible which illustrate suffering by chastisement for sin and suffering according to the will of God. Read the story of Jonah and the storm in Jonah chapter 1 and the story of Paul and the storm in Acts 27. Then study the following chart:

Jonah	Paul
Jonah put himself in the storm	Paul was in it through no fault of his own
He paid the fare to sail	He tried to prevent them from sailing
He was the cause of the storm	He was the remedy, not the cause
Jonah slept during the storm	Paul fasted and prayed
God's blessing was not with Jonah	God's blessing was with Paul
The crew was fearful	The crew was of good cheer
To be saved: Jonah must be cast out of the ship	To be saved: All must abide in the ship

There are differences between going through a storm of life within God's will and experiencing a storm out of the will of God. When you go through a storm out of the will of God, it is a situation which you create. For example, a believer who marries an unsaved person will experience trouble because they have violated a Scriptural principle.

When you cause a storm, it is because you violate God's will and are disobedient to His commands. Often you are not even aware of the seriousness of your situation. You sleep spiritually while the storm increases its fury around you. God's blessing is not on you, and those around you grow fearful. This storm is not an attack of Satan. It is chastisement from God who loves you and desires to bring you back into conformity to His will. You can confess promises of "power over the enemy" but it will not change the situation.

When you recognize a storm of suffering as one resulting from disobeying God's voice, there is only one remedy: Ask forgiveness from God!

But when you suffer according to the will of God, the situation is different. You suffer through no fault or sin of your own. You can be a remedy to the problems around you instead of a cause. Like Paul, you can assume spiritual leadership because God's blessing is on you. You can bring encouragement to others because you are a solution to the storm instead of the cause. You should not bail out of the ship or run from the trouble. You must abide in the "ship" of this type of suffering for it is the will of God.

SUFFERING IS TO BE EXPECTED

When you suffer according to the will of God, you should realize you are not alone:

> **. . .knowing that the same afflictions are accomplished in your brethren that are in the world. (I Peter 5:9)**

Storms of life are inevitable and uncontrollable, as illustrated by the parable of the two houses in Matthew 7:24-27. Storms will come to those who have built their lives upon God's Word as well as those who have not done so. The foundation of a man's life is what will determine the outcome of the storm.

Suffering is to be expected as part of the will of God:

> **Yea, and all that will live godly in Christ Jesus shall suffer persecution. (II Timothy 3:12)**

> **For unto you it is given in the behalf of Christ, not only to believe on Him, but also to suffer for His sake. (Philippians 1:29)**

> **. . .that ye may be counted worthy of the Kingdom of God, for which ye also suffer. . . (II Thessalonians 1:5)**

> **For verily, when we were with you, we told you before that we should suffer tribulation; even as it came to pass and ye know. (I Thessalonians 3:4)**

> **Then shall they deliver you up to be afflicted, and shall kill you: and ye shall be hated of all nations for my name's sake. (Matthew 24:9)**

> **. . .they shall lay their hands on you, and persecute you, delivering you up to the synagogues, and into prisons, being brought before kings and rulers for my names sake. (Luke 21:12)**

> **Remember the word that I said unto you, The servant is not greater than his lord. If they have persecuted me, they will also persecute you. . . (John 15:20)**

Part of the follow up plan in establishing early churches was to teach believers that they would experience suffering. This is missing in many churches today:

> **. . .They returned. . .confirming the souls of the disciples, and exhorting them to continue in the faith, and that we must through much tribulation enter the kingdom of God. (Acts 14:22)**

The call of Jesus to followers is one of denial and suffering:

> **And he that taketh not his cross, and followeth after me, is not worthy of me. (Matthew 10:38)**
>
> **Then said Jesus unto his disciples, If any man will come after me, let him deny himself and take up his cross and follow me. (Matthew 16:24)**
>
> **. . .Whosoever will come after me, let him deny himself and take up his cross, and follow me. (Mark 8:34)**
>
> **. . .come, take up the cross, and follow me. (Mark 10:21)**
>
> **If any man will come after me, let him deny himself, and take up his cross daily, and follow me. (Luke 9:23)**
>
> **And whosoever doth not bear his cross, and come after me, cannot be my disciple. (Luke 14:27)**

WHEN THE BROOK RUNS DRY

There is an interesting Old Testament story of a man who experienced suffering within the will of God. That is the story of Elijah. Elijah experienced all types of suffering as he prophesied God's message of Israel. But the particular story we want to focus on is found in I Kings 17. Read this story in your Bible before continuing with the lesson.

When God first directed Elijah to the Brook Cherith, He provided for him miraculously. Ravens came to feed him, and the brook provided fresh water in a time when the nation was experiencing drought and famine. But eventually, the brook dried up. Why would God send Elijah to a brook He knew would dry up?

The will of God sometimes involves dry brooks. But when we experience such difficulties it does not mean we missed God's will. Elijah had not missed the will of God. The Lord led Elijah to Cherith. He enjoyed its waters. His needs were provided. He was blessed of God. But when it was time to move on, God allowed the brook to dry up. This got Elijah's attention.

Perhaps God has directed you to a "Brook Cherith" in life. You know you heard His voice of direction. He blessed you at your brook. Your needs were met and you rejoiced in God's blessings. But then the brook ran dry. Maybe you no longer experienced the flow of God's power. Perhaps people turned against you. Perhaps leadership above you dammed up the brook and stopped the flow. For whatever reason, your beautiful brook ran dry.

When the brook runs dry you can do one of two things:

1.	You can sit on the bank spiritually speaking and complain about your fate. You can spend the rest of your life wondering why it happened and weeping over the dry creek bed. You can question the leading of God. Did He even bring you here in the first place? If He knew the brook was going to run dry, why would He have brought you here? Did you miss God's will? Or. . .

2.	You can realize that as surely as God brought you to this brook, He is now ready to move you on to a new dimension of His will. He is gaining your attention through the dry brook.

If brooks never dried up. . .if God never let difficult times come. . .He would never get our attention. Like Elijah, we would settle right where we are and never move on to new things. We would never stray beyond the banks of security of our brook. Drying brooks lead to greater things. Before the experience at Cherith Elijah had ministered only to individuals. After this faith-building encounter, Elijah ministered to multitudes. He stood on Mt. Carmel and proclaimed before a nation of idolaters that God was the true and living God.

When you face drying brooks, your faith must not fail. You are on the banks of receiving new revelation from God. Do not question dry creek beds. Move on to the next dimension of God's plan.

SELF TEST

1. Write the Key Verse from memory.

_____

_____

_____

2. What are five ways suffering may enter the life of a believer?

_____

_____

_____

_____

3. List three positive benefits of suffering according to the will of God.

_____

_____

_____

4. List three of the positive attitudes the believer is to have when experiencing suffering:

_____

_____

_____

5. Read the following statements. If the statement is True, write the letter T on the blank in front of it. If the statement is False, write the letter F on the blank in front of it.

a._____It is never God's will for you to suffer.

b._____If you experience trouble it means you are out of the will of God.

c._____Paul was out of the will of God in the storm at sea which he experienced.

d._____When you suffer out of the will of God you are often the cause of your own problems because of disobedience.

e._____God chastises you because He loves you and desires to bring you back into conformity to His will.

f._____If Elijah had been in God's will by going to Brook Cherith, the brook never would have run dry.

g.____God sometimes uses trouble to get your attention because He wants to lead you in a new direction.

h.____The Bible teaches only sinners experience suffering.

(Answers to tests are provided at the conclusion of the final chapter in this manual.)

FOR FURTHER STUDY

1. Study the book of I Peter which focuses on the subject of suffering. Record what you learn about suffering from this epistle:

    _____

    _____

    _____

2. Study the following references about suffering:

    HARDNESS:

    II Timothy 2:3

    TRIBULATION:

    Acts 14:20; Romans 5:3; 12:12; I Thessalonians 3:4, II Thessalonians 1:4

    PERSECUTION:

    Matthew 5:10-12, 44; 13:21; Mark 4:17; Luke 11:49; 21:12; John 15:20; I Corinthians 4:12; II Corinthians 4:9; Acts 8:1; 11:19; 13:50; II Timothy 3:12; Romans 8:35; Galatians 6:12

    SUFFERING:

    I Peter 5:10; Philippians 1:29; 3:8; 4:12; II Corinthians 1:6; II Timothy 2:12; 3:12; Galatians 5:11; 6:12; Acts 9:16; I Thessalonians 3:4; II Thessalonians 1:5

    AFFLICTION:

    Psalms 34:19; 119:67,71,75; Matthew 24:9; Acts 20:23; II Corinthians 2:4; 4:17; 6:4; I Thessalonians 3:3; II Timothy 1:8; 3:11; 4:5; II Corinthians 1:6; James 5:10; Hebrews 10:32-33 and chapter 11

CHAPTER TWELVE

SIX STAGES OF REVELATION

OBJECTIVES:

Upon completion of this chapter you will be able to:

- Write the Key Verse from memory.
- List six stages of the revelation of a plan of God.
- Identify this pattern in Biblical examples.

KEY VERSE:

> **And thine ears shall hear a word behind thee, saying, this is the way, walk ye in it, when ye turn to the right hand and when ye turn to the left. (Isaiah 30:21)**

INTRODUCTION

In this course you have learned much about knowing God's voice. You learned prerequisites for knowing God's voice. You learned the meaning and pattern of God's will and ways in which God communicates with man.

You were warned of non-Biblical ways of seeking guidance and received guidelines for making decisions regarding questionable practices. You studied a Biblical model for decision making and learned what to do when you fail. You also studied about suffering as it is related to God's will.

This final chapter presents the six stages through which you will pass in the revelation of a plan of God. You will experience these stages as you learn to walk in the will of God.

REVELATION KNOWLEDGE

In a confused and misdirected world, God promises revelation knowledge to His followers. This means He will reveal divine plans, wisdom, and knowledge in the circumstances of life:

> **And thine ears shall hear a word behind thee, saying, this is the way, walk ye in it, when ye turn to the right hand and when ye turn to the left. (Isaiah 30:21)**

When God reveals a plan, there are six stages through which you pass in the development of that revelation. These stages are evident in Luke 1:26-47. Read this passage before continuing with the remainder of this lesson. These Scriptures record the revelation of God given to Mary that she was to become the mother of the Messiah, Jesus Christ.

In this story there are six stages through which Mary passes as God's plan is revealed to her. These stages may be observed in the revelation of any plan of God to man. They are stages through which you will pass as you receive revelation knowledge of His plan for your life.

STAGE ONE: VEXATION

And the angel came in unto her. . .and when she saw him, she was troubled at his saying and cast in her mind what manner of salutation this should be. (Luke 1:28-29)

When the angel first appeared to Mary, she was troubled or vexed in her spirit. Whenever God wants to give new guidance, you often experience vexation. He permits you to be troubled by the circumstances of life in order to gain your attention.

Perhaps you are questioning perplexing circumstances around you. You have been troubled and not understood why certain things were happening to upset your life. God is trying to gain your attention. If you are happy and content in present circumstances you will not seek Him for new direction. This is why He allows you to be troubled in this first stage of revelation.

STAGE TWO: REVELATION

And the angel said unto her, Fear not, Mary; for thou hast found favor with God.

And behold, thou shalt conceive in thy womb and bring forth a son and shalt call His name Jesus. (Luke 1:30-31)

When God gains your attention through vexation, He will reveal His plan to you. This is the second stage of revelation:

Call upon me and I will answer thee, and shew thee great and mighty things which thou knowest not. (Jeremiah 33:3)

A troubled spirit caused Mary to focus her attention on God then He revealed His plan. She was to be the mother of the Messiah, Jesus Christ.

STAGE THREE: HESITATION

Then said Mary unto the angel, How shall this be, seeing I know not a man? (Luke 1:34)

Mary hesitates to accept this great revelation. She questions, "How can this be?"

When God reveals new direction for your life you are often overwhelmed. You may feel unqualified. You may feel it is too great a step of faith to take. You will think of rational reasons why the plan cannot work. You will hesitate and question God.

Two things happen in the stage of hesitation:

-You present your questions, reasons, and excuses.
-God answers these with details of His plan.

Some people hesitate longer than others. Some people spend years in the hesitation stage thinking up excuses and reasons why they cannot accept the revelation God has given. But if you do not eventually move on from hesitation you will never see the fulfillment of God's revelation.

STAGE FOUR: RESIGNATION

And Mary said, Behold the handmaid of the Lord; be it unto me according to thy word. . . (Luke 1:38)

Mary moves quickly from hesitation to resignation to the plan of God. This means she resigns her will to God's plan. She gives up her own plans and desires and accepts God's new direction for her life.

STAGE FIVE: VERIFICATION

And blessed is she that believed; for there shall be a performance of those things which were told her from the Lord. (Luke 1:45)

In the verification stage, God verifies or confirms His plan. Mary becomes pregnant and the revelation is verified in her own body. If you resign your will to the revelation of God's plan, it will not be long until you receive verification of that plan.

STAGE SIX: EXALTATION

And Mary said, My soul doth magnify the Lord. (Luke 1:46)

Mary rejoices in the plan of God! Read her complete exaltation of God in Luke 1:46-55. When you accept the plan of God for your life it will always bring happiness and result in exaltation of God.

As you learned in this course, following God's plan does not mean you will be without problems. In the natural world, Mary had a real problem. She was pregnant without being married. But the plan of God is greater than any temporary suffering which it involves. In the end, it always brings joy and exaltation of the Lord Jesus Christ.

A FINAL WORD--LISTEN FOR HIS VOICE

In this course you have received guidelines for knowing the voice of God. As you listen for this voice, remember His promise:

> **. . .I know the thoughts and plans that I have for you, says the Lord, thoughts and plans for welfare and peace, and not for evil, to give you hope in your final outcome. (Jeremiah 29:11, The Amplified Version)**

God will continue to guide you until death:

> **For this God is our God for ever and ever: He will be our guide even unto death. (Psalms 48:14)**

His guidance will continue in the new heaven and earth:

> **For the Lamb which is in the midst of the throne, shall feed them, and shall lead them unto living fountains of waters; and God shall wipe away all tears from their eyes. (Revelation 7:17)**

God is not silent. If you listen, His voice can be heard above the noise and confusion of all the voices of earth. God speaks and you can know His voice:

> **Now the God of peace, that brought again from the dead our Lord Jesus, that great shepherd of the sheep, through the blood of the everlasting covenant,**
>
> **Make you perfect in every good work TO DO HIS WILL, working in you that which is well pleasing in His sight, through Jesus Christ; to whom be glory forever and ever. Amen. (Hebrews 13:20-21)**

SELF-TEST

1.   Write the Key Verse from memory.

_____

_____

_____

_____

2.   List the six stages of revelation of a plan of God.

_____

_____

_____

_____

_____

_____

(Answers to tests are provided at the conclusion of the final chapter in this manual.)

FOR FURTHER STUDY

Study the pattern of the six stages of revelation in the lives of Moses and Gideon:

Moses:	**Exodus 1-15**
Vexation:	Experienced in Egypt (killed an Egyptian)
Revelation:	Burning bush
Hesitation:	Man of slow speech
Resignation:	Decides to go
Verification:	Miracles before Pharaoh
Exaltation:	Joy after crossing Red Sea

Gideon:	**Judges 6**
Vexation:	Threshing wheat; pours out vexation in verse 13
Revelation:	Angel appeared in verse 12 and 14
Hesitation:	"Family poor, I am the least" verse 15
Resignation:	Verse 17
Verification:	"Shew me a sign" verses 17 through 23
Exaltation:	Verse 24. Builds an altar and praises God.

Can you find other examples of this pattern in God's Word?

ANSWERS TO SELF-TESTS

CHAPTER ONE:

1. My sheep hear my voice, and I know them, and they follow me. (John 10:27)

2. The "rhema" word of God is the life-giving word communicated to meet a specific need. It can come through the written Word of God, a sermon, spiritual gifts, or through an inner voice in your spirit.

3. The "logos" Word of God is the written Word of God contained in the Holy Bible. Nothing is to be added to or taken from it.

4. If you come to know His voice, you will know His will as He speaks it to you.

5. Hebrews 3:7 or 15.

6. The general plan of God for your life, guidance in making wise choices, and direction for the circumstances of life.

7. It always agrees with the "logos" or written Word of God as recorded in the Holy Bible.

8. Sin.

9. Doer . . . hearer.

CHAPTER TWO:

1. I beseech you therefore brethren, by the mercies of God, that you present your bodies a living sacrifice, holy, acceptable unto God, which is your reasonable service.

    And be not conformed to this world; but be ye transformed by the renewing of your mind, that ye may prove what is that good, and acceptable, and perfect will of God. (Romans 12:1-2)

2. Prerequisite means something you are required to do before you can do something else.

3. Prerequisites for knowing the voice of God include: Born-again experience, Indwelling of the Holy Spirit, Spiritual maturity, and Transformation.

4. Guidance. The Holy Spirit reveals God's will by speaking it into your inner spirit.

5. To acknowledge you are a sinner, confess your sins, repent, and accept Jesus Christ as your Savior.

6. You must have a personal relationship with God in order to come to know His voice.

7. It means to gain maturity in things pertaining to the spiritual world, to grow spiritually.

8. To be changed into another image, patterned after the Lord Jesus Christ.

9. The statement is true. See Romans 12:1-2.

CHAPTER THREE:

1. For I came down from Heaven not to do mine own will, but the will of Him that sent me. (John 6:38)

2. Love.

3. Review the reasons listed in Chapter Three.

4. A choice or determination of one having power.

5. Sovereign (boulema), individual (thelema), and moral.

6. Self-will, Satan's will, God's will.
7. a. False; b. True; c. False; d. True; e. False

CHAPTER FOUR:

1. O Lord, I know that the way of man is not in himself: It is not in man that walketh to direct his steps. (Jeremiah 10:23)

2. The word "emulations" means copying others in order to equal or excel them. It stems from a spirit of rivalry and is a form of jealousy.

3. a. False; b. False; c. False; d. True; e. False; f. False; g. True; h. True; i. True

CHAPTER FIVE:

1.   Having made known unto us the mystery of His will, according to the good pleasure which He hath purposed in Himself;

    That in the dispensation of the fulness of times He might gather together in one all things in Christ, both which are in Heaven, and which are on earth; even in Him;

    In whom also we have obtained an inheritance, being predestinated according to the purpose of Him who worketh all things after the counsel of His own will. (Ephesians 1:9-11)

2.   The two divisions of God's will discussed in this chapter are that which is revealed in His written Word and that which is not revealed in His written Word.

3.   The principle that would apply to this decision is found in II Corinthians 6:14-15. Believers are not to be yoked together with unbelievers.

4.   God wants you to know His will.
God's will is planned.
God's plan is individual and personal.
God's plan is progressive.
God's will is not man's way.
God's will is good.

5.   False.

6.   Diagram A.

7.   Perfect will, Good will, Acceptable will, Out of God's will.

CHAPTER SIX:

1.   Be ye not unwise, but understanding what the will of the Lord is. (Ephesians 5:17)

2.   Any one of the following could be used: Moses and the rock; Elijah on the mountain; Philip and his trip to Samaria; David and his two encounters with giants.

3.

Written Word of God	Miracles
Prayer	Dreams
Counselors	Visions
Circumstances	Audible Voice
Closed and open doors	Inner voice of the Holy Spirit
Angels	Gifts of the Holy Spirit

4.   a. False; b. False; c. False; d. False; e. True; f. True

CHAPTER SEVEN:

1.   Trust in the Lord with all thine heart; and lean not to thine own understanding. In all thy ways acknowledge Him and He shall direct thy paths. (Proverbs 3:5-6)

2.   Peace.

3.   See Proverbs 3:5-6

4.   To reflect God in thought, word, and deed. To give Him first place in your life.

5.   Pray.
        Search the Scriptures.
        Listen to the inner voice of the Holy Spirit.
        Seek Christian counsel.
        Analyze the circumstances.
        Use Biblical keys for direction.
        Choose the way of wisdom.

6.   a. False; b. False; c. False

CHAPTER EIGHT:

1.   Whether therefore ye eat, or drink, or whatsoever ye do, do all to the glory of God. (I Corinthians 10:31)

2.   Questionable practices are activities or behaviors not specifically mentioned in God's Word as being either right or wrong.

3.   Does it glorify God?
        What is your motivation?
        Is it necessary?
        Will it promote spiritual growth?
        Is it an enslaving habit?
        Is it a compromise?
        Will it lead to temptation?
        Does it give the appearance of evil?
        Does it violate your conscience?
        How will it affect others?

4.	A "weaker brother" is a believer who, because of weakness of faith, knowledge, or conscience can be affected by the example of a stronger brother. He can be influenced to sin against his conscience or his spiritual progress can be hindered.

5.	A "stronger" believer is one who, because of his understanding of freedom in certain areas and the strength of his conviction, exercises liberty with good conscience. He is not influenced by the differing opinions of others.

6.	Distinguish between matters of command and freedom.
	Cultivate your own convictions.
	Allow others freedom to determine their own convictions.
	Limit liberty by love.
	Resolve all offenses.

7.	Go to him alone. If it is not resolved . . .
	Go again and take one or two witnesses with you. If it is not resolved . . .
	Take the matter before the church.

CHAPTER NINE:

1.	A man's heart deviseth his way; but the Lord directeth his steps. (Proverbs 16:9)

2.	A model provides an example for you to follow.

3.	A model for decision making is an example to follow when making choices.

CHAPTER TEN:

1.	Oh, that my people had hearkened unto me and Israel had walked in my ways. (Psalms 81:13)

2.	Study these again in Chapter Ten.

3.	Study these again in Chapter Ten.

4.	Recognize your failure.
	Repent.
	Recognize the departure point.
	Return to correct the error.
	Revelation: Seek God for and act upon new direction.

CHAPTER ELEVEN:

1.   Wherefore let them that suffer according to the will of God, commit the keeping of their souls to Him in well doing as unto a faithful creator. (I Peter 4:19)

2.   Others around you.
Circumstances of life.
Your ministry.
Direct Satanic activity.
Your own sin.

3.   See the benefits of suffering discussed in Chapter Eleven.

4.   See the attitudes towards sufferings discussed in Chapter Eleven.

5.   a. False; b. False; c. False; d. True; e. True; f. False; g. True; h. False;

CHAPTER TWELVE:

1.   And thine ears shall hear a word behind thee, saying, this is the way, walk ye in it, when ye turn to the right hand and when ye turn to the left. (Isaiah 30:21)

2.   Vexation, Revelation, Hesitation, Resignation, Verification, Exaltation

www.ingramcontent.com/pod-product-compliance
Lightning Source LLC
Chambersburg PA
CBHW080517090426
42734CB00015B/3090